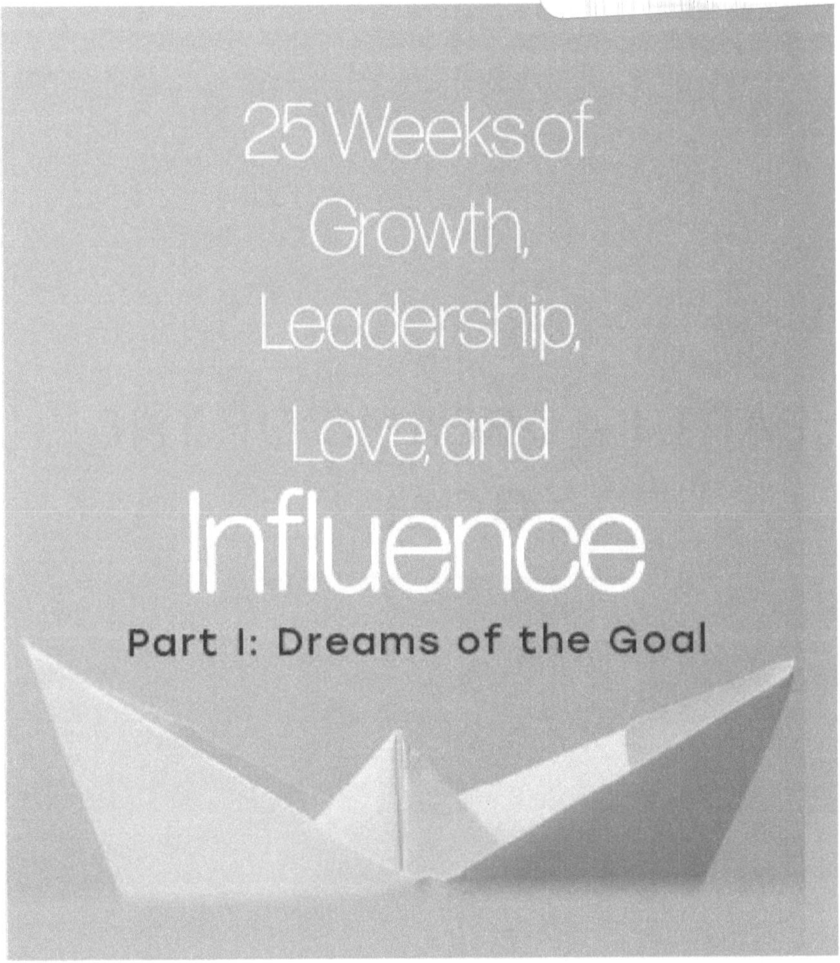

25 Weeks of Growth, Leadership, Love, and Influence

Part I: Dreams of the Goal

Copyright © 2023 by Jerica M Richardson

PART I – DREAMS OF THE GOAL

This book is dedicated to my readers in pursuit of personal growth.

Preface

The Journey

About the Book and the Author's Intention

Influence can be a very tricky thing when trying to learn how to wield it. However, you can unlock your passions, dreams, and potential by simply learning how to influence yourself and those around you. I have put this book together as a much simpler approach to my more robust textbook-novel "Influence" because my passion is to help empower others to understand themselves, discover their purpose, and to embrace their inherent power.

Over the next 25 weeks, I encourage you to approach one chapter per week and 1) dissect, 2) reflect, 3) meditate, and 4) practice on the lessons and stories that ensue. The content was originally developed for ivory-tower members of academia, but I wanted to make sure that these tools were accessible to the masses. I have used them throughout my career in mentorship of others. It does not matter your status in this world, how you were born, or who you know. You have EVERYTHING you need to become the full expression of yourself.

First things first...

There are topics that will be discussed in this book that may cause some discomfort, but that is the content's attempt to stretch your way of thinking – broaden your horizon and challenge your limitations. Influence always begins with exploring how much you know yourself, your preferences, desires, tendencies, etc. Some of us seek power, and some of us equate that word to corruption. Some say influence, some say manipulation. We ascribe feelings and perceptions to words that may sometimes prevent us from gaining further knowledge because we are afraid that it challenges our ideals. I am fully aware that my readers are not of the same thought or background. So, as you read, try to remain as open as possible so that you hold a true mirror to yourself. Because influence can be used for good or ill intent, I have a few housekeeping rules that I hope you embrace as we proceed through the chapters.

Standards of Leadership:

- *Allow each day to present me with a learning experience.*
- *Remain receptive to all points of view because truth is embedded in everything.*
- *Continuously mold myself into becoming my best.*
- *Carry myself with dignity.*
- *Accept the consequences of my actions.*
- *Resume responsibility for my character.*
- *Love my fellow person.*
- *Distract my attention from gossip and stereotypes.*
- *Believe in the greatest ability of myself and others.*
- *Become a role model for my community.*

If you can embrace these thoughts, I believe you will be well on your way to a balanced approach in embracing your inner strength and aptitude to influence.

The Approach:

In the original book, there are 5 themes, each with 5 chapters. We will retain this structure for this version as it helps to describe the journey upon which you are about to take part.

Within this book, there are 5 chapters dedicated to achieving the desired end state as described by the theme summaries above.

I have organized each chapter in the following way:
   a) Key Definitions & Terms
   b) Lessons Tenets
   c) Lesson Exercises
   d) Week's Meditation Tenets

For every chapter, you can also visit the website to find videos and testimonials related to the corresponding lesson.

I truly hope you are excited about your journey. It is one I continue to be on as I move throughout this life and am happy to have you come along as well!

The book was compiled in a manner that would allow you to really be aware that both leadership and personal development take time and involve a process of evolution. There are stages, but the stages may involve different things for different people. I have confidence that this book will meet you halfway, regardless of how you may look at life. Remember that it takes time and focus to reach your goals, and that advice can be fitting for whatever you may be pursuing.

Part One Introduction

Dreams of the Goal

A dream can represent your greatest desire for success. Your goal is to pull from the deepest corners of your sense of self and clearly visualize, from beginning to end, the dreams you hold. In this theme, you will be tasked with focusing on crafting the big picture and identifying how a purpose or role fits into a larger one.

In today's device-driven world, we find ourselves looking down significantly more than in the past. We see it in fatal car accidents and harmless street walking collisions. Occasionally lifting your eyes to the horizon, however, will keep you from such a collision. Moreso, when it comes to your dreams, it will allow you to anticipate impending circumstances and properly prepare for them. These challenges may help you, hinder you, or do nothing at all; but by recognizing them you will know how to gauge them, direct them, and properly respond to them if you keep looking forward.

So, what does this mean in a practical sense?

It means having awareness about your surroundings and an understanding of other people. Perhaps you would like to become an engineer, a doctor, an entrepreneur, or work in one among many other important jobs that will supply a steady foundation for you and a sense of job security. Specifically, when you are considering a potential career track, it is imperative to keep in mind the prospective qualities of the job as there are many careers that once existed just to vanish thirty years later. For all dreams, take note as to whether you are willing to make the sacrifices needed to succeed in that career or life goal. If you are not, chances are, it is not something you subconsciously want to pursue, and you will find yourself taking that tend to prevent or sabotage your progress. Part One helps you identify and define what it means to have a career or life goal and forces you to contemplate which sacrifices are necessary. Truth is that you likely do not realize you already have all the answers you need, but now, it is time to be honest and diligent about your present and your future. When you dream of your goals, you partake in the process of making them a reality because you will have made the dream as realistic as possible.

There are many inspirational quotes you can gather from different sources. Wealthy and wise leaders of humankind's past have all offered many. Pick one that describes who you are and make it your temporary motto. Keep it in mind as you read the next five chapters. It will keep your spirits high, and you will place the necessary personal context in each of the following lessons.

Week **One**

The purpose of this week is to understand and define leadership, the motivations required to have maximum success, and to demonstrate what contributes to determining your leadership activities.

Roles of Leadership

Note: *"What is a leader? I see it as the biggest multitasker on the team. The leader has to do a number of things efficiently and effectively."* **(Young Leader)**

Yes, being skilled in multi-tasking is an important quality to embrace. As you go through life, many affairs are going to require your attention. Your friends and family, schooling, extracurricular activities, career, community service, and of course your own well-being will all have a share on your list of preoccupations. Within each of these categories, there are different considerations. At any job, you may be required to answer phones, schedule meetings, maintain great working relationships, complete your tasks and or goals, find ways to improve your work performance, and tend to your health so that you can be physically prepared for your job. Anyone who says that multi-tasking is unnecessary is a part of another world.

Certainly, as we move into a more connected and technologically savvy society, multitasking is a skill that you might as well accept as a necessary part of life. The caveat with multitasking is not being able to understand the tricks to doing it well, and what should and should not be multitasked. We will attempt to dissect that later this week, but for now, let's take a closer look at references to effectiveness and efficiency.

As a leader, which we will define, it is also important that you understand there will be many influences and facets to your success.

The operational definitions for this chapter are below:

Leadership is deemed as the position or function of a leader. A leader has the ability to lead. Leadership is an act or instance of leading, guidance, and providing direction.

Effectiveness has several important meanings including an actual operation or force; the effort adequate to accomplish a purpose or producing the intended or expected result; it also means to produce a deep or vivid impression; it means to be prepared and available for service.

Efficiency is a notion that can only be discussed when considering the amount of effort invested. It is the ratio that exists between the energy developed versus the energy invested.

In the definition of leadership, note that leadership is identified as the position or function of a leader. The term 'leading' for the purposes of this chapter, means guiding or moving in a particular direction. So, putting the two together, when you are in the function of guiding, then you are, in effect, leading. When you offer advice as a friend, a consultant, or head of an organization, you are leading. You are using tools of communication and products of your own thoughts to try to convince yourself or another person of a belief. When a group of people are seated in one room, each one assumes a specific position, usually self-determined. The interactions that follow are the manifestations of these self-determined roles, and a good leader understands how these interactions are related to what each person thinks and believes.

The second proposed definition is that of effectiveness. If your leadership is to portray effectiveness, then it must be operational. It is encouraged that it produces an intentional effect. Intentional effectiveness is rooted in the idea that there is a certain amount of premeditation to your actions. If you are not intentional in your actions, then you will find yourself encountering a series of seemingly unpredictable circumstances. While it may be a fun way to experience your life, it is not a good method to use if you aim to be effective. It is quite ineffective, and you will lose the confidence of others if you are leading a team. The definition also describes effective as producing a deep or vivid image. This should be your way of measuring your effectiveness. Are you able to communicate and deliver an idea with a lasting impression? The views that leave an impression on us are usually provocative in nature and appeal to the basic human sense of love, hope, or fear.

The final definition for effectiveness introduces the idea of service. As a servant leader, you are subject to your decisions. Your decision to participate or disengage, or to move east or west will ultimately paint the picture of your leadership. To what degree do you acknowledge the things to which you are a servant to? Being subject to your decisions means that you understand who and what your decisions affect and that you consider those factors in the decision-making process. Asking questions such as, "Who am I helping?" may begin to open the door to your understanding of your servant leadership.

The last operational definition for this week is for the term efficiency. When determining efficient leadership, recognize that efficiency can only be determined when an initial amount of energy is expended. This means you should be ready to work as a leader. This leadership energy is expended in the form of reflecting, creating, thinking, deciding, and/or executing. Efficiency, in engineering terms, is the ratio of energy output to the energy invested or total energy available.

In summary, think, "Out of what is accessible, what has been produced?" Efficiency requires thinking outside of the box and envisioning a new method to accomplish a task with the greatest output. This is analogous to society's incessant search for new energy sources as an example. Fossil fuels, nuclear, and coal, all produce different efficiencies, and their effectiveness considers the consequences for each method's relative efficiency.

As a leader in the information age, you should consider a few things...

I.   **You are always expected to be a leader.**

Under all circumstances, expect that you will have to be accountable for your actions and their consequences. Recognize that in all situations, you have made decisions and consequently have participated in the act of leading. Instead of using the pervasive notion of "leading" with respect to leading other people, use the idea that the simple act of deciding is "leading". You are leading yourself. When you decide to speak out, it is because you decide that what you have to say is merited. The *choice* to sit back, whether consciously or subconsciously, is still a choice made by you. An effective leader considers the possible consequences that can occur from a decision and considers what is influencing the decision. An efficient leader then thinks, decides, and acts on what he or she deems is the best course of action. You must begin at step one, however, and realize that all you do and where you are, is the sum of the many decisions you have made throughout your life. Taking accountability in that facet will open the door for you to begin to identify the causes and effects of those decisions. This is where there is potential for growth and where you can decide to pursue the goals that you dream of.

So, in all troubles, begin leading by asking, "What part of it was my fault, and what could I have prevented?" At the end of the day, each person is responsible for his or her own actions. This is not because we can't be there for one another, but rather it has more to do with the idea that most must and are concerned with their own well-being, so much so that if they have any energy remaining, then they may be concerned for the welfare of others. Simply put, relying on the availability of others is not always an efficient choice. So, now that you know you are always expected to be a leader, what does that mean in the context of how you think, decide, and execute?

Composure

"Law 35 -Master the Art of Timing -Never seem to be in a hurry – hurrying betrays a lack of control over yourself, and over time. Always seem patient, as if you know that everything will come to you eventually. Become a detective of the right moment; sniff out the spirit of the times, the trends that will carry you to power.

Learn to stand back when the time is not yet ripe, and to strike fiercely when it has reached fruition." **(48 LAWS OF POWER)**

    A.   <u>Understand your surroundings.</u>

The 48 Laws of Power by Robert Greene is a very straight-forward literary work that avoids sugar coating truths. As indicated by the quote, composure is critical to your ability to manifest and display power. Composure affords you the space and time to effectively interpret your surroundings. Composure is a key component to your leadership. When you are leading a group or yourself, maintaining a clear and focused mind is going to help you navigate through unfamiliar territory. Being in a hurry physically or mentally will betray your ability to focus. Outwardly, your displayed anxiety also decreases the trust and faith that you and others have in your ability to be effective. By maintaining composure, you will be able to manage expectations and recognize important contextual clues in your surroundings. It is important to not be so distracted by unfamiliarity that you miss what is occurring around you. If you become overly entangled in the mechanics of your job performance or your academics, you will miss the other opportunities that may enhance your experiences and potentially bolster your career or academic status. For example, if you are in a class and are solely focused on the material that you are learning, without gaining clarity of what is expected, you will place unnecessary and unexpected limitations on your performance. Clarity on placed expectations is just as significant as the knowledge you bring to every test. Not understanding the rules of the classroom is like trying to play chess with Monopoly's rules. Perhaps you are studying management. By taking advantage of an internship or a mentor in the field, you will gain perspective on what you do in the classroom and vice versa.

Alternatively, perhaps you are in an office setting, and you neglect to meet with your superior for clarity on expectations in advance of a meeting. Perhaps you have discounted the value of befriending your colleagues and your superior. In these scenarios, it matters little what your presentation is, because you were unable to understand your surroundings. Practicing composure would mean taking information in first through listening and observing. So, when the team meeting actually occurs, you can display the same kind of corresponding composure to your audience. You can get a *feel* for what is expected. Keep in mind that people recommend, hire, and promote those they trust. Knowing the vision of the company you work for will accelerate your progress and add layers of satisfaction to your job routine.

Take a moment to reflect on your dreams of the goal. Take the time to consider and understand your goals, objectives, the job market, other people, influences, and opportunities. You will gain a definite advantage by adopting the practice of effective and efficient leadership. Each day the world changes in how it processes information, handles intelligence, and engages in business. Contrary to what others may purport, you must adapt to multi-tasking at this level.

In the effort to exhibit composure, please note that the basic wants and needs of people do not really change. Most people seek to firstly have security for themselves and their families and then secondly to satisfy the ego. You can use this to your advantage, and it will help when trying to understand more complex systems. Similarly, the struggle between security and ego may also be a distraction in your personal life and cause you to lose your composure. When observing your surroundings, keep these things in mind.

Composure Exercise: Think of an area of life that creates anxiety. Meditate on which aspects threaten your security and shift your attention to the contributing factors. Which needs of others involved are at play? Are they behaving in a way that is disruptive due to a challenge on their security or ego?

[Some situations require a specialist and that is not covered in the scope of this book, but there are some resources that you may want to review at the end of this book.]

Pride and Ignorance

"A proud spirit, therefore, is deadly to leaders. It will kill their effectiveness ... for it breeds two dreadful diseases of the soul. The first is ignorance. Pride makes a person self-sufficient and unteachable. It blinds them to their own needs. It causes them to ignore the good advice and counsel of others." **(BE THE LEADER YOU WERE MEANT TO BE)**

    B.   <u>Identify your leadership weakness (es).</u>

This process is the most laborious of them all. How do you go about identifying your weaknesses? Everyone is great at offering advice but trying to find the weaknesses is another concept all in itself. The quote suggests an insightful way by which you can accomplish this. Pride and ignorance are two very distracting elements. In life, you will encounter awful circumstances, and you must be willing to learn from each one. You will also have to learn from the experiences that offer you great joy.

Train yourself to think about what you are experiencing while you are amid emotional moments. Instead of letting your pride betray you, use it to predict the responses of your own ego and the ego of others.

Reflect on the list of what you are prideful about. When others tell you "You are such a great ---- or such a handsome man or woman", do you feel a sense of encouragement? If so, it qualifies as an asset you are prideful of. Make a list of these qualifiers. This is the first half of your list of weaknesses. Keep in mind that at some point, all weaknesses will be used against you. Referencing the example above, you can sense that your vanity is reliant upon another person's subjectivity. There is no shame in it, but by knowing that someone can gain your trust by offering a compliment will help you better sort through another person's motivations in offering a compliment. These vulnerabilities will be used against you. Understanding what you are prideful about opens a window to what others are prideful about, because people function based on similar social cues.

Ignorance is the manifestation of using your own ideals as a comprehensive standard. It is our main way of offering judgment to others. While your convictions may be true and unwavering, they may not be true to someone else, rendering you ignorant of who they are and their expectations. It allows them to use your own idealistic standards against you. If ignorance is the blind acceptance of your idealistic standards to the exclusion of others, then the words used to describe these standards can be noted as "judgment words". When you use adjectives, they are the judgments you are delivering. Even if they are readily accepted as applicable, they are still judgments, i.e. 'The sky is blue'. Use judgment words to identify your ignorance. You can gain insight into your perspective of the world, as language reflects thoughts. To better understand what this means, you can refer to what takes place in a courtroom. Lawyers spend their time trying to convince a jury of the *innocence* of a client and the *faulty* claims of the other party. They appeal to the jury's sense of *justice* and *mercy*. The lawyer uses many judgment words that have been accepted as true. When defending the client, they use judgment words that compel the jury to believe or trust the client. 'Fairness', 'righteousness', and 'justice' are commonly used. Rarely is the list of facts void of any adjectives or nouns with strong connotations. Lawyers lead the conversation with vividly described images. Perhaps the defendant was *wrongly* hurt, or the *unknowing* child should be cleared of all possible punishments. Lawyers appeal to the ideals of others through vivid retelling of scenarios and characters; otherwise, they are sure to lose the sentiments of the jury. As for the judge, a good lawyer is also aware of the surroundings and works the system to find the most sympathetic jury and the "fairest" judge. Be aware of the judgments you make in your mind and use this to gauge how you think. You can better understand others by identifying their judgments.

Identify the judgment words you use to describe yourself and the world and add them to your list of weaknesses. Take note that anything can be used as a weakness, but they are not as easy to identify as what you may or may not be good at doing. Many times, the things you are not good at are manifestations of your judgment words (ignorance) and of what you are prideful.

> Pride and Ignorance Exercise: Run through what was described in this section of the chapter. Knowing which words you use to describe your skills and personality will certainly bring insight into how you perceive the world as well. By writing these standards

and confronting them, it will be easier to recognize when someone is disagreeing with them. After committing your list of pride and ignorance to your mind, listen carefully during your next conversation. Try to listen for what the other person is really communicating to you about your relationship.

Attention

"Everything is judged by its appearance; what is unseen counts for nothing. Never let yourself get lost in the crowd, then, or buried in oblivion. Stand out. Be conspicuous, at all costs. Make yourself a magnet of attention by appearing larger, more colorful, more mysterious, than the bland and timid masses." **(48 LAWS OF POWER)**

    C.   <u>Opportunities are everywhere.</u>

In the first section, I asked that you pay attention to your surroundings with composure. Something quite spectacular occurs when you consciously choose to do so. When you are focused on a particular outcome or goal, and aware of your surroundings, the right opportunities become remarkably prominent. It is almost as if a yellow brick road paved itself with the exact steps you must take. When you seize these available opportunities, note that you will draw attention to yourself.

While attracting attention may stir up your fears, others will begin to place their trust in you and expect you to live up to certain standards. Keep in mind this is why you must maintain composure, and this is the way to push your personal progress. Imagine if you decide you want to help others. If you are never actually affecting others, how can you accomplish what you set out to accomplish? When you are pursuing your goals with fervor and focus, people will recognize it and help work to make it happen. Many scientists have contributed to our current technological era, but only a few are noted for their discoveries. Even fewer have discovered something with obvious commercial applications. The others fall into an unacknowledged oblivion alongside their most promising works. What would happen to the scientist that never gets funding for a project? What would happen to a presidential candidate who received no media attention but wanted to advocate and help design laws that would save the country? How could the candidate accomplish what he or she set out to do if that candidate never took advantage of the systems in place to allow for a successful campaign? Not only does the candidate lose, but they also lose the opportunity to affect the country, and the scientist loses the opportunity to make any advancement.

Drawing attention to your effort does not mean that you must sacrifice your own standards or morals to impact the world. Instead, the goal is to have a vivid and intentional vision by which you can utilize your standards and elevate them to the point where the goal is achievable.

Imagine you are in a crowd of people shouting at one person on a stage, and you begin to shout alongside them. In this scenario, each person is shouting something different. Will the person on stage be able to discern what you are shouting? On the other hand, you could hold a poster or sign with your words or find a way to be the only person doing the shouting. Maybe you can wear a ridiculous outfit that causes the crowd and the listener to spot you. All these options will yield a different result than simply shouting alongside the crowd. In practice, perhaps your method of standing out in the conventional way is not actually allowing you to function as an individual who brings value to a situation. Rethink the opportunities you have taken advantage of and perhaps whether they have brought about the correct attention for you to continue towards success. When applying for law school your application needs to stand out. In a job interview, the employer must feel he or she trusts you and to do that, you must stand out. Beware that, when it comes to drawing attention to yourself, you must be strategic, thoughtful, and careful. What you stand out for and how you stand out are just as important as standing out. (The 48 Laws of Power also discuss the importance of guarding your reputation.)

Make it your goal to stay ahead of a curve by doing two things: counting your blessings and paying close attention to trends. As we move into a smaller, more accessible, and complex world, the way business is conducted, and the manner by which ideas are shared changes every day. So, maintain a clear mind in recognizing trends in jobs, services, and products. In business school, a corollary can be found in product life cycles and anticipating future technologies. Getting a job selling VCRs may not be lucrative today but being on the cutting edge of robotics or computer modeling systems may yield substantial monetary gains within the near future. All jobs, services, and products have life cycles. It is your responsibility to understand the cycles and factor them into identifying potential opportunities.

For finding the right opportunities, realize that situations may not be as they seem. How you interpret a situation will guide you to a certain conclusion, so it would be wise to be mindful of what influences you and your weaknesses as described above. When interpreting situations, you can only use the background knowledge you have. The brain functions by developing what are known as schemas. Schemas are patterns or groups that the brain uses so that it can determine how to appropriately respond in a very short amount of time. How you were raised, your religious or non-religious background, the people you have encountered, the information you have acquired, and what you have been told about your position in society, each affect the schemas you develop. Take the time to identify and understand your schemas by reflecting on your reactions and actions in moments of danger, failure, accomplishment, and love. After identifying your schemas, realize that the motivation to pursue and identify opportunities stems from them.

As you begin to be more intentional about the opportunities you seek, consider that there are a few fundamental concepts that should form the foundation of your journey. These are known as standards. Standards will allow you to determine whether you are deviating from your sense of principle and idealism. You will have the opportunity to create your own in addition to those introduced in this chapter and embody them as principles in later chapters.

> Attention Exercise: Think of an area of life that creates anxiety. Meditate on which aspects threaten your security and shift your attention to the contributing factors. Which needs of others involved are at play? Are they behaving in a way that is disruptive due to a challenge on their security or ego?

Standards

Allow each day to present me with a learning experience.
Remain receptive to all points of view because truth is embedded in everything.

Continuously mold myself into becoming my best.
Carry myself with dignity.
Accept the consequences of my actions.
Resume responsibility for my character.
Love my fellow person.
Distract my attention from gossip and stereotypes.
Believe in the greatest ability of myself and others.
Become a role model for my community.

    D.   <u>Expect yourself to live up to the Standards of Leadership.</u>

The Standards of Leadership listed is meant to provide a blueprint for the standards that you will create. These are open and vague enough to begin. They are further described below.

Allowing each day to present a new learning experience is vital to your growth. You encounter new information and perspectives every day. Do not take these for granted. When you are in the midst of a new experience, be present and embrace that you are encountering this experience in real time. There exists an opportunity to grow, but you must be focused enough to recognize it.

Remain receptive to all points of view because truth is embedded in everything. Adopting this principle is a bit tricky. It does not mean that everything should be recognized as true. It implies that everything is true for someone. In any given statement, even within a lie, there is truth in discovering the intention of the lie. The fact that a person lies indicates that other unapparent thoughts occurring compel the person to decide to lie. Therefore, that individual had to accept certain beliefs as true for them to arrive at lying to be the most viable and acceptable option. In essence, it means that people only do things once they have justified it for themselves. Understanding that and how it affects judgments will create room for freedom in your ability to predict and engage others- especially when it comes to their needs.

Continuously molding yourself into becoming your best means that you should have no moment of true boredom. If you constantly evaluate and reflect upon your weaknesses and the new experiences life creates for you, you will see yourself evolve. By using this as a standard, you will find that each day will bring about a different and more refined "you". So, in your studies, try to identify the habit you could enhance or avoid. If there is something you wish you did more of, just do it. Of course, it takes more than just verbally deciding to change. You must focus on your motivations and determine why you currently do or do not do something. By starting at this point, you can then change your habits.

Carry yourself with dignity. This is imperative. You should be poised in your decisions and should live with little to no regret. Hindsight is 20/20, but in the moment, you made the best decision you could have possibly made. You should reflect on preventing poor decisions and acknowledge when you have wronged someone but be sure to maintain your sense of dignity with your admission.

Accept the consequences of your actions. This should go without saying, especially within the definition of leadership. Once you grasp the idea that you are always expected to be a leader because you are always making decisions, the next step is to recognize how your decisions directly tie to consequences. Life will never stop treating you as a leader. You should fully accept the consequences. You should be aware of your shortcomings, faults, and ignorance, as you will ultimately be indebted to them. If you do not have the tenacity to be responsible, even if it is secretly, you will never learn from others. You will find yourself repeating the same errors many times over.

Resume responsibility for your character. The implication using the word "resume" is that taking responsibility for an error is a process. Even within the circumstance of a mistake, you must continue to take responsibility for your character. As for your character, you must know what makes you quick to anger, extremely happy, or insatiably jealous. Then, you must take full responsibility for your shortcomings. Errors are not just in an action but are also in your personality, or rather your reactions and responses. Perhaps you find yourself blaming the messenger or demeaning others. There will certainly be consequences for how you make others feel in addition to what you do to or for others. It behooves you to become familiar with these flaws, embrace them, and understand where they come from so that you can begin your refinement process.

Love your fellow man/woman. Under all circumstances, you should respect other people for who they are and where they are. Every individual is comprised of desirable and undesirable qualities. Taking the moment to understand another individual will do more wonders than any form of coercion. Understanding someone does not indicate that you agree with their stance. It simply means that you can determine the judgments and rationalizations that a person used to arrive at their state. Respect is a very high form of love, and you will gain access to your dreams by offering it to others. You should never treat someone in a manner that is inconsistent with who they are. They will always fall short of that expectation.

Distract your attention from gossip and stereotypes. Participating in these activities will always end up with someone getting hurt. Most likely, that someone will eventually be you. Gossip and stereotypes, in this list, are classified as false statements or fallible conclusions that are used to identify or categorize others. By using false statements or fallible conclusions, you will be led to a false sense of confidence and any invested work will prove to be ineffective. Do not confuse causation with correlation when it comes to classifying others. It is indeed a setup for you to lose yourself and your opportunities.

Believe in the greatest ability of yourself and others. Hope for the best but prepare for the worst. You should not rely on others to perform to impress you, but rather only to perform in a way that satisfies their own egos. When someone does not perform up to their actual potential, believe that the person has the capability to perform but has not been properly incentivized or placed in the appropriate situation to generate such outcomes. With this mindset, you can see where your shortcomings are and how to garner the most out of your leadership.

Finally, become a role model for your community. When others encounter you, an archetype should come to their minds. How you are perceived, how you look, and your brand, should deliver the same message. For whichever activities you are engaged in, aim to become the model for that activity. This is how it should be done. Keep in mind that while others may not be inclined to help you, they are still watching you, and gathering information about what to do.

So, to add the altruistic flair to this entire book, make sure you are setting a standard that is good for the world, and not bad for the world. It will be the last impression you give when you go to the grave. Also, keep in mind that when you pass away, the standards you possessed will leave an empty mold that someone else will come to occupy.

These standards are suggested mainly because the tools and tricks that are discussed in this book can be used to really benefit the world but can also create incredible harm. The tools of leadership are neutral, but the intentions behind your actions will ultimately influence the outcomes. Follow the standards of leadership you set for yourself and let them become your daily measuring tool.

II.   If you are a leader, then you have followers.

This may be the oft most forgotten part of leadership. There are people following you. If you are leading yourself, then you are also following your own decisions. That is what it means to follow your own path or define your own life. You define how you will live by your decisions. Taking the time to really understand your followers and your ability to follow will help in matters of rebellion, discovery, development, connection, and achievement. There are some very important characteristics to being a follower and being a leader with followers.

> Standards Exercise: What beliefs do you hold about new ideas? What ethical standards are important to you? Think of a tense situation you recently experienced, and consider what you deemed to be important? Did you want to be right? Did you rather to be effective? Did you react or did you respond? Then, ask yourself why. Also, take a moment to reflect on the proposed standards at the beginning of this section. What do they mean, which do you do, which do you reject which resonate with you?

Then, ask why and write down the ones you most desire to encompass.

Hierarchy

"This principle embodies the truth that there is always a correspondence between the laws and phenomena of the various planes of Being and Life. The old Hermetic axiom ran in these words: 'As above, so below; as below, so above'." **(Kybalion)**

    A.   <u>Followers will mimic their leaders.</u>

The Kybalion can be quite esoteric in its explanations of worldly things, but the basic premise is that the parts of the whole, to some extent, exemplify the whole. If an organization is viewed as a moving body, much can be learned about the leaders by speaking with the followers. Much can be learned about the followers when a discussion is prompted with the leaders. When there is a disconnection between the leaders and the followers, it further provides insight into the kind of leadership the person at the top possesses. We also deem the organization 'disorganized' because of the dissonance. It manifests itself in a practical sense in the form of deviation from reality – disorganized paperwork, documentation, overworking, under-planning, lack of strategy and more. As for the quote, it plays on the idea that in the same way dysfunction and success occurs on lower levels, it also occurs at higher levels. Smaller organizations combat the same issues that larger organizations do. The difference is in the scale and the complexity. The unforeseen elements to these issues and complexities are known as emergent properties. Emergent properties are properties that are evident in the entirety of an organization, organism, or system but are not displayed by the individual elements that make it up. Much will be said about this Correspondence Principle in later chapters. With regards to this chapter, however, it is important to keep in mind that when accomplishing something well, hierarchy becomes a pivotal aspect to strategic implementation. Each person has a role and while roles should be of equal importance, they do not share the same burdens of responsibility, nor do they consist of similar methods or volume of work.

Imagine a child learning to walk, which words to say, or facial expressions to make. The child takes cues from the parents. Did that person smile and make me feel good? I should do it again. Did that action give me a response I liked? I should do it again! It really is as simple as that interaction. We read social cues to determine whether something is acceptable, and these back-and-forth interactions continuously build and morph our schemas as discussed earlier. This is important because in part it allows others to feel comfortable around you. We are comfortable with things, people, and experiences we can anticipate or predict. Change presents potential unknown variables and may result in our dissatisfaction. When dealing with people on both small and large levels, this holds true. Only the scale of interaction is different. So, within some organizations, you may find elements of uniqueness but for the most part, we eventually mimic or rebel against those to whom we must answer.

Imitation is the highest form of flattery. Each person longs to feel some form of acceptance and belonging because humans are social creatures. If a person shows no want for acceptance, then there are perhaps other considerations that need to be made. Generally, there is a desire to be acknowledged by some kind of authority. This could be an organizational leader, parent, or supervisor in your leadership journey, it would be wise to note that when followers "mimic" their leaders (this is both in rebellion and in imitation), it is usually in seeking specific attention or acknowledgment. You can respond to this need by listening, providing a platform, or rendering an award. This is true on any level of the hierarchy. Even the CEO of a company must answer to his shareholders. When a CEO and Chairman cannot account for a large amount of lost money, not only do shareholders want answers, but the public also demands some sense of accountability to be forced into the banking industry.

Likewise, if you choose to shame your leaders, you put yourself at risk of losing their respect and loyalty because you are disrupting hierarchical principles. Note that rebellion is imminent, as it will be fueled both by the need to satisfy the ego and by the need to be secure.

> Hierarchy Exercise: Take the time to reflect on all that influences you. Think of organizations you have participated in. How does the organization structure impact its ability to thrive and make decisions? Spend time reflecting on how the organization is structured; many times, we join a company or entity without fully understanding its structure. Even the country you live within has a governing structure. If you do not know how it is structured, how authorities are separated, where accountabilities exist, and how decisions are finalized, or which parameters decisions must abide by then, you are at a severe disadvantage. So, use this as an opportunity to map those entities you are a part of and how their authority and powers are derived. If you cannot find it on your own, then ask someone.

Loyalty

"Work on the Hearts and Minds of Others -Coercion creates a reaction that will eventually work against you. You must seduce others into wanting to move in your direction. A person you have seduced becomes your loyal pawn. And the way to seduce others is to operate on their individual psychologies and weaknesses. Soften up the resistant by working on their emotions, playing on what they hold dear and what they fear. Ignore the hearts and minds of others and they will grow to hate you." **(48 LAWS OF POWER)**

    B.   <u>Understand your followers.</u>

To properly work on the hearts and minds of others, you must take the time to understand others. When you cannot understand the rationalizations of another person, it is the same as being ignorant to them. You have heard the idea of "walking a mile in another man's shoes". This adage encompasses what it means to truly understand others. What are their weaknesses? What are their desires? What are their fears? By answering these questions, you will gain insight into the motivations of those around you as well as yourself. In marketing, if you appeal to basic needs or convince someone that a specific item or service is important to them, then that person can become loyal to you, your cause, or your product. If you do not take the time to understand others, however, you will find that your efforts to accomplish anything will yield a fruitless garden. Animosity will overcome your followers and they will rebel against whatever you have to offer. This is true even of ideas that are meant to benefit others. Your leadership will come to ruin if you betray the trust of those who follow you. Remember, at a minimum, you are always leading yourself, and that ideas that are true are true at scale. So, understanding followers does not just apply when you are leading a group of people. It also applies to when you are leading yourself. If you go against your individual psychology, you will find execution very difficult. Thus, it is just as important, if not more, to take the time to understand yourself as a follower.

When you communicate with others, be sure to include one or both concerns in the context: ego or security. For example, money is something that appeals to both needs. "Ego" deals with a person's sense of belonging or desire, while "Security" encompasses physical and emotional safety. When these needs are satisfied, you can gain the loyalty of others. When communicating to others' needs of security and ego, you must give a little of yourself so that the person you are speaking with feels more comfortable about what you are offering. If you want to find out someone's motivations, reveal a little about your own, and their doors will be wide open for further discussion. How you reveal your motivations is an art. If your motivation is to cause harm or discomfort, you will not meet the security needs of your audience. When you draw someone outside of their comfort zone, they then must trust you to lead them, or guide them. Their security and ego depend on your good decisions. You can imagine this kind of interaction in this way:

You convince a person that they must be blindfolded while you guide them through a forest. You explain that you are guiding them towards a pot filled with money. You tell them that the blindfold is needed to make sure that they stay protected and not be distracted from your guidance by the musings of the forest. If you do this correctly, any person will willingly be blindfolded and guided by you through the forest at your advice. People will do this because they feel they will retrieve what they feel they deserve. They have been influenced and their needs understood.

> Loyalty Exercise: Many times, we have people who are truly loyal to us, but they are underappreciated. Think of everyone who you have worked with or connected with. Pick one person that you are not sure of where their loyalties exist for this exercise. Do you know what motivates them? Do you know what they fear? How have you used that information to demonstrate your knowledge of who they are? Have you offended them by actualizing any of their fears? Have you relayed information in a way that was disrespectful to their ability to receive information? Are their motivations contrary to your objectives? You will likely find that the incongruencies cause you to innately question their loyalty. Now, pick a person who is loyal and consider the same questions. At all times, you should be aware of the loyalties of those in your circle by conducting this exercise.

Control

This curriculum stresses internal unity (discourse with oneself) and external unity (discourse with others). In order to accomplish this type of harmony, the curriculum focuses on four dimensions of our lives: physical, spiritual, social, and mental. [Being a member simply] means that you will live in harmony with the principles of StartUp: focus, power in expression, strength, individuality, and creativity. **(STARTUP CURRICULUM)**

C. <u>Be an effective and efficient leader and follower.</u>

Not only must you embrace opportunities, and learn to listen to others, but it is also important that you can describe your leadership. Effective and efficient are meant to reflect the definitions provided at the beginning of this chapter. While the above statement may be metaphorical in nature, it simply means that obtaining self-control requires being able to predict your own actions. What are your vulnerabilities and what are your strengths? Under which circumstances will you thrive, and in which activities should you participate? The act of following and leading requires the avoidance of pride and ignorance becoming weaknesses. You must master your emotions and understand how to use them to elicit desired effects. Of course, this kind of introspection will only occur after you accept and envision yourself as always in the act of leading. This is one of the first decisions you must make!

As for the "dimension" reference, it is a suggestion for how you can view the world. These dimensions will be further explained in Week Three, but they refer to four tiers: social, physical, mental, and the spiritual. The spiritual in this sense deals with motivations and experiences. It is where one gains their reasons for persistence. These tiers go all the way to the social which includes how the rest of society interacts with the object or person under observation. As an apple tree bears apples that other entities consume, so does a person have creations with which other entities will interact. When you perceive something, you are observing, making assumptions, analyzing, and drawing conclusions on it. You repeat this cycle for events recognized as being similar and modify your conclusions accordingly. This culminates in your world perception, and you start identifying ways in which your world may be improved based upon how you see it. The idea here is to fully understand your world view so that you can see how it fits into other perspectives. By thinking as broadly as possible, you free yourself to comprehend the world through many lenses.

With this, you will have the ability to be effective and efficient because not only are you considering other possibilities, but you are also implementing solutions. This is an important characteristic of leadership. It is the main difference between self-authorized leadership and title-authorized leadership. Both offer authority, but self-authorized leadership includes the idea of participating in some position of influence, while maintaining appropriateness and leading with accordance to a vision. It requires imperatives designed and motivated by you.

The other important take-away from the opening quote is the idea of focus. Focus is different from narrow-mindedness. Focus means that you are concentrated on some fixed point. This does not mean you will not have to multi-task. To maintain proper perspective on your current circumstances, there must be some amount of focus on your end-goal. When you focus on your end-goal, you consider the other factors that may influence the end-goal. Do your current activities bring you closer to your focus? Think of a diagram concerning lenses and optics. The focus is a point of convergence. It is where everything can culminate to one point. Depending on whom you are and your lens, the focus point will be different.

III. **Your Leadership must have a purpose.**

You should clearly define and envision your end goals. Hopefully, you are not simply in a position of leadership, but that you are committed to leading. It is not called leading otherwise, and you are just occupying space and engaging in title-authorized leadership. If there is no rhyme or reason to your decision-making, then you are leading without a purpose. If this is the case, beware that you will be replaced very soon. There must be some marginally added value to your presence as a leader. Perhaps it is to discover new territory or to improve the internal organization of a larger system. Perhaps it is to bring great credit to your supervisor. What will your leadership bring to the table? If you do not determine your leadership's purpose, there is certainly the off chance that you may haphazardly bring value. However, there is no efficiency in that route. In haphazardly producing results, you will miss valuable opportunities because you lack control and misunderstand those around you.

> Control Exercise: Regardless of your situation, make the decision that you are a leader. List one attribute you would like to express as a leader, and ask these questions: Do you currently exhibit this trait? Why do you want to exhibit this trait? Why do you agree with this explanation? What circumstance in the near future will allow you to demonstrate this trait? What are the consequences of exhibiting that trait? Would others agree with your assessment? Why or why not? Do you still agree with your decision to exhibit this trait? What fuels your conviction? For others that have exhibited that trait, would you be interested in the life they have because of it? Why or why not? Now, imagine yourself going through the upcoming situation where you have demonstrated that trait. How do you feel? How is your physiology? Does it stress

you? If so, why? Does it make you joyful? If so, why? Does it make you feel accomplished? If so, why?

That is what it is like to experience control over your thoughts and feelings and lead yourself.

Ambition

"I want to put a dent in the universe."

(STEVE JOBS)

A. <u>A purpose is a destination.</u>

Finding your purpose seems to be somewhat of an elusive endeavor, and it always seems like something that is a goal beyond reach or hard to determine. Well, do not get too caught up in trying to find the perfect word or phrase to describe your purpose. Just think of it as a destination. When you see yourself as an older individual, what are some of the things you would hope to have accomplished or become? What characteristics do you possess? These are destinations. Take a moment and envision yourself in that space. When you can clearly feel, visualize, and hear everything that is involved with your destination, it is as if you mentally highlight the path that may get you there. Whenever you are confronted with a decision to make, you should firstly imagine your destination. You should also imagine the different opportunities and challenges that you will encounter regarding all the options and see if you are ready for the kind of sacrifices that will most likely come with your decision.

If you do not imagine your leadership with a purpose, it is as reckless as going on a road trip with a map in which you cannot read the streets nor have a destination in mind. Sure, the ride may be thrilling, but you will pass by all the turns that could take you to a place you would really want to visit. Those streets are the opportunities for growth, and the destination is your purpose. As a matter of fact, if you decide to drive blindly, you will encounter more challenges and many of them will be unnecessary. Something to be wary of - if you make a turn that is too far in the wrong direction, it may prematurely end your road trip for you and whoever else chose to come along for the ride.

In the quote, Steve Jobs makes a proclamation of putting a dent in the universe. While this goal may be a bit vague-sounding or too metaphorical in nature, it still gets the point across. It becomes a standard. Are my current activities going to lead me to cause change that feels big enough to leave a dent in the universe, or am I falling in line with the natural flow of the world? For Steve Jobs, these questions would have produced great reflections on whether 'a dent is being made in the universe.' What do you want to do? What is your destination, and what are you doing to get there? Are your activities bold enough? Without that stated purpose, you would have no point of reference to check whether you are moving in the direction that best represents who you are.

Take note that even this book has an intended purpose-

Objective: *My concern is to ensure the growth and development of each person who reads this book. The focus is to help you determine your purpose and make sure that you have the resources necessary to fulfill your purpose. (J.M. Richardson)*

This is the objective or the destination of this book. It may happen that you complete the rest of the chapters and find that you have not been affected at all. That is a choice. You must decide to be affected and dedicate the appropriate time to personal and professional development.

> Ambition Exercise: What does success look like for you? Make a list of concrete objectives and/or visuals that represent how you would like to be and act. Then ask yourself, what would the world be missing without you? We will develop this answer over the next few weeks.

Meditation Tenets

A river stays in constant motion but is restful in its winding maneuvers. Honest to itself in search for the path of least resistance; turbulent when disturbed, it contains within it the secret to life and death.

Below are some questions that you should not quickly come to an answer for, but rather find some time to reflect upon. Consider the meaning of these questions (some have multiple meanings), and then meditate on your answers. When you have found your answer, it should feel honest and consistent with who you are.

1. What are the standards you choose to adopt and why?
2. Do you think of yourself as a leader? Why or why not?
3. Who leads you and who follows you? Why?
4. What decisions have brought you to your current lot in life?
5. What are you currently seeking to accomplish? What does the next step look like for you?

6. What are some things that others seek to gain from you and why?
7. What are some things that you seek to give to yourself?
8. When was the last time you felt hopeful? Why?
9. What about uncertainty scares you?
10. Have you considered your purpose and are you engaging in activities that help you accomplish it?

Week **Two**

This week's chapter demonstrates that leadership is the sum of a series of moments that require leadership. The description of leadership follows directly from the previous chapter. The chapter goes on to explore how your overall leadership abilities are affected by those moments, and the way they should be perceived.

Moments of Leadership

Note: *"The race will free itself from exploiters just as soon as it decides to do so. No one else can accomplish this task for the race. It must plan and do for itself."* (MIS-EDUCATION OF THE NEGRO)

The story of man exploiting man is a very old one. It is wise to assume that history will repeat itself as it already has so many times. The idea of this chapter is that you must understand that in every moment, you can learn something about your inhibitions and your liberties. Experiences and beliefs truly shape how well you survive. Cultures and groups with a strong identity rooted in historical importance or tradition will find themselves lasting from one generation to the next more often than not. As much as we may not like to admit it, a group's ability to self-determine its identity affects the individual moving parts of that group's expectations, experiences, and beliefs. Many studies have been used to show the effect that experiences and culture can have on behavior. Something to keep in mind is that the world is becoming a more mixed one. With such mixing, there will be a period of cultural clashing that will eventually evolve into immersion. Language, mannerisms, and expectations currently vary by wide margins, but expect this to continuously evolve as time unfolds. The world will be a more accessible entity, and almost nothing will occur in a vacuum. This is an even more reason to pay attention to the context in which you are defining yourself.

Imagine the opening quote with "the race" being replaced with the words "you" and replacing "It" to "you". Much can be gathered from this statement.

If you need some assistance, here's how it would read:

"You will free yourself from exploiters just as soon as you decide to do so. No one else can accomplish this task for you. You must plan and do for yourself."

Assume that the only person in this world that cares about you is yourself. Others are consumed by their needs and wants. Therefore, if something is going to happen for you, or if you are going to lead something, then the keyword here is "you". If you make an error, you will have to assume responsibility and do your best to avoid issues. Now, it is not true that your good works will occur solely because of your effort. Cause and effect relationships affect more than general events but are directly involved in influencing your success.

There are always many levels of participants in a successful venture. This statement simply urges you not to rely on another individual and apply pressure when you can leverage a specific outcome. When engaging in applying pressure, remember your standards. If you are doing unjust harm to an individual to appease your ego or security needs, chances are you will face proportionally excessive consequences for your crimes. (The reason behind the excessiveness will be because rebellion is fueled by irrational emotions.) As you are making your way on your journey, remind yourself that your circumstances are of your doing. This is not for you to preach to another, but it should be the platform on which you begin to reflect on those moments of leadership that have ultimately led you to your current state.

The other important aspect of this quote is the idea of decision making. With discrimination or slavery there are some very significant psychological tools at play. If one takes the time to read history, for either to properly work, the individual discriminated against must be convinced that discrimination is appropriate, necessary, immutable, and therefore inevitable. These tools of superiority psychology are so powerful that they have affected generations of people. If the individual does not subscribe to a mindset, however, then he or she will rebel against it in their own unique ways. It works the same way in your life.

For you to operate under a certain mindset, it is simply because you have accepted it to be true. What are some of the paradigms with which you currently live? What do you consider to be unchangeable and inevitable? If you are not content with your current circumstances, you must accept that it was a series of your choices that contributed to them. You are accepting your situation and the responsibility thereof. The operational definition for this chapter is below:

A <u>moment</u> can be defined in many ways, but the most captivating is thus: a definite period.

People make judgments based upon what they see. So, your leadership is represented by the *moments* in which you were required to demonstrate your leadership. These moments can either be presented to you or created by you, but you must take advantage of them and use them to help you strive toward your purpose. Carpe diem, anyone?

Things to consider if you are a leader...

I. **I will be required to testify to my beliefs.**

There are many ideals that we ascribe to ourselves. We like to see ourselves in a light that is usually unblemished and steady. We would like to believe that we are great or perfect, and so when it comes to our decisions, we frequently practice a certain amount of self-righteousness. This is not a bad thing and proof that there is a confidence that exists in the core of who we are as individuals even when we do not feel so confident. It's evident because we feel empowered to decide in the first place. We choose to wake up, try again, have a difficult conversation, try something new, clean up, clear something up, and on and on. A consequence of our confidence, however, can make it hard to admit to wrongdoing or an improper choice. We also find it hard to forgive others who make a choice different from ours. We find ourselves saying "I would never do that" or "how could you accuse me of doing that". This stubbornness may be effective for friends and family, but there will be days where you will be forced to handle the repercussions of such obstinacy. By not recognizing your potential to commit a crime or act pretentiously, you will fail to control yourself when the opportunity occurs. Trust, if everyone could live and function the way they imagined themselves to, then the world would truly be a better place.

Acknowledging that you could hurt *and* help is the first step to self-control. If you continue to be naïve about your nature, there will be a day when your greatest weaknesses will be tempted. If you believe you are capable of owning or managing a business, or mingling with a large crowd of individuals, be sure to understand why you believe that, and whether you truly believe your proclaimed belief, because life will come quite fast.

Sense of Self

"Each day look into your conscience and amend your faults; if you fail in this duty you will be untrue to the Knowledge and Reason that are within you." **(A SPIRITUAL TREASURY)**

    A.   <u>I will have to lead myself.</u>

One of the moments to developing your leadership is the one you spend contemplating yourself. What makes you happy, or sad? What do you fear and what do you love? What are your insecurities and where did they come from? Answering these questions will help you understand what drives your decisions and will help you prepare for situations that may affect you in an otherwise unforeseen way. In all situations, the responsibility of a decision rests upon you, and you will eventually receive and deal with the consequences of the emotions that occupy your mind. If you are too fearful of failure, then you will find yourself always debating the best-case scenario that causes the least amount of resistance.

So, if fear drives you more than love, you may lose out on the things you claim to want because the fear of the prospective consequences clearly outweighs the love of success. You can avoid many errors and cornered defeats by fully understanding yourself. The truth is that other people will take the time to understand you, even if you do not. So, while you are pretending to possess few weaknesses, your friends and enemies are becoming aware of your quips and quirks and will be able to influence you in ways that will result in your eventual feeling of powerlessness. You will be tested by others, and at those moments, your true beliefs will be revealed.

It is imperative that you understand that you are always expected to be a leader and that there will be moments when your leadership will be tested and defined based upon the results. Imagine the circumstance of a young startup CEO searching for seed funds who finds himself sharing one untruth. To maintain his appearance of credibility, out of fear of rejection, he must continue to be dishonest. Each of these moments define his tenure, legacy, and destination. The lies will erode the confidence others may have once had in him, and he will eventually become exactly what he was afraid of becoming. He would be rejected by the community. Had he understood what was motivating him, he could have prevented those consequences.

> Sense of Self Exercise: What motivates your decisions? Think of the last 5 decisions you have made – was it personal health, wealth, comfort, achievement, etc. Make a list of what you would like to motivate your decisions, and under which circumstances each is appropriate. Are you consistent with this list? If not, then why?

Growth

"Have you ever visited a pottery factory? When the pottery is placed in the kiln, its colors are dull and muted. After it has been in the fire- when it comes out of the oven-its colors are vivid." **(Be the Leader you were Meant to Be)**

    B.   <u>I will face very difficult times.</u>

Along with moments of testifying to your beliefs, there will be moments that are filled with heat and pressure. These moments, however, are opportunities for success. You should gladly welcome them as challenges to prove to yourself who you are. These pressurized moments should push you to your breaking point, and if you prepare wisely, you will prevail and be better for it. You will be more useful, polished, and valuable, as is a crystal.

The other key takeaway from the above quote is time. It takes time to reach a mature form. You should always be malleable but convicted. Conviction is by principle and malleability is by understanding. Conviction and stubbornness differ by the width of understanding. You can erase your stubbornness by understanding the perceptions of others. As aforementioned, possessing the ability to understand others and yourself will allow you to grow. Pride can be an unwanted result of having convictions. The best safeguard here is to keep an open mind that others also have their convictions, and that your standards are not the world's standards. Practice by trying to "justify" another's beliefs. This exercise will yield you greater insight into your own convictions as well. Your connection to your surrounding community is a special one.

The more you take the time to understand others, the more you will understand yourself.

II.   I must seek my opportunities for leadership.

The image of someone wanting to prove their strength comes to mind. He may go from one place to another, initiating fights to show others that they should fear him, and revere him for his strength. As primal as it sounds, it is exactly what we do. Our resumes are a list of fights that we have participated in, and hopefully won. We go from one opportunity to another seeking to prove ourselves to ourselves and to others. Be cautious of the fights that you pick. They should reflect exactly what you want to be known for. This does not mean to defer a job because it is not what you see yourself doing, but it means that if you take that job, shape the job so that it matches who you are. Create an opportunity within the opportunity. This is the recommended process for seeking opportunities.

While you are actively making decisions that will position you for opportunities, realize that serendipity does play a vital role in the presentation of an opportunity. Something to keep in mind, however, is that moments of serendipity occur many times over time and expose you to an abundance of opportunities at any given time. It is upon you to identify and leverage that opportunity. It can be said that you do not notice just how many blue cars are on the road until you have a blue car, or someone sparks up a conversation regarding blue cars. We miss our opportunities hundreds of times a day!

Growth Exercise: When was the last time you sought an opportunity to lead or make a decision? What is something you want to accomplish today? What opportunity can you create to move in that direction today? Write it down and seek out that opportunity.

Perspective

"Said one oyster to a neighboring oyster, 'I have a very great pain within me. It is heavy and round, and I am in distress'. And the other oyster replied with haughty complacence, 'Praise be to the heavens and to the sea, I have no pain within me. I am well and whole both within and without.' At that moment a crab was passing by and heard the two oysters, and he said, 'Yes you are well and whole; but the pain that your neighbor bears is a pearl of exceeding beauty.' **(A Spiritual Treasury)**

    A.   <u>Obstacles are opportunities for success.</u>

Recognizing potential opportunities is crucial to potentiating and leveraging them. So, what kinds of opportunities might we be missing? According to the story, the oyster with the pain could only recognize the pain, and not the beauty of what that pain could produce. You must train yourself so that you can see every obstacle as an opportunity. If you find yourself doubting your capabilities to overcome a difficult problem, take the time to step back and evaluate what may come from triumphing over the presented obstacle. As a matter of fact, having an end goal in mind will allow you to prepare yourself for opportunities disguising themselves as obstacles.

The result of learning through an obstacle is that you have a story and can then proceed to more difficult and complex problems. In a nutshell, you become more useful as an individual, and as a leader. Use an obstacle as an opportunity to find mentors. In the story, if the crab had not told him the reason for the pain and the outcome of its endurance, the oyster would have been left to complain and miss its value.

Think about the events that have occurred in your life. Understand that each situation is a consequence of other situations, and that each has shaped how you look at life, and how you handle new circumstances. Imagine if you had never encountered those experiences. What would you value then? What might you be doing differently? What habits might you have developed? After reflecting on those questions, you will gain some perspective on how your life has been pieced together, and you will be able to comprehend how obstacles are truly opportunities for success.

> Perspective Exercise: What is something that has occurred in your past that you had control over and did not like the outcome. In what ways can the outcome be used to your advantage? Are you able to connect to someone because of your story or understand where another person is coming from? How can that be used to help you achieve something today?

Sequence

"Every Cause has its Effect, and every Effect has its Cause; everything happens according to Law; Chance is but a name for

Law not recognized; there are many planes of causation, but nothing escapes the Law." **(KYBALION)**

    B.   <u>Any decision you make has a cascading effect over time.</u>

Order and chaos are simply degrees apart representing a spectrum of system organization. System order describes the degree to which each of the elements connects or relates to one another. If you want to run for office in the United States of America, a particularly *ordered* route may be:

1. Be born into a wealthy family with a background in public office.
2. Go to a school where you can maintain a network of family friends who also have a background in public office.
3. Intern for someone in public office
4. Attend a prestigious college and affiliate yourself with a political party.
5. Obtain a law degree and maintain relationships with others who are involved in public policy or public office.
6. Develop a unique record of success in your profession.
7. Create professional relationships.
8. Run for local office in your area.

This example demonstrates intentional order. As you read this list, however, you may have had thoughts like, "How can I control which family I am born into?", "How can you just go to a prestigious school?",

"Would not I need money to do some of these things?", or "How would I just work for someone in public office?" You are so right! These are uncontrollable factors. Instead of such an ordered list, you are subject to chance and opportunity. In that light, life is chaotic. So, then things must be unconnected or unrelated, right? However, this section is about the importance of sequence in life. It means that if A happens, then B must happen. Because B happened, C will happen. If you read this book, then the book is read. These connections are infinitesimally small, but they add up yielding a multitude of orders. By itself, an order is predictable and guaranteed. Humorously, when these orders interact with one another, the result is perceivably chaotic.

Chaos could be described as the result of everyone's "order" working and colliding with one another. These unpredictable factors for some are simply the injection of the order by others. This is important to take note of because as you make decisions, like the leader that you are, you will be subject to what seems to be chaos. The trick is to understand the orders that are interacting with one another and perhaps you will be able to make predictions that could impress Nostradamus. So, you can stack your deck by becoming an expert in systems – or interacting orders. These systems could be concrete: business cycles, engineering processes, or policy tracks. They could also be more intangible: human emotions, human behavior, or human actions. Not to mention, you have the occasional flamethrower who aspires to stimulate chaos within order. Understand how these systems interact with one another and how each system is connected.

Because you have an aptitude and desire for an end goal (a destination), this sort of high-level thinking will help you keep perspective, which in turn will help you find opportunities in situations that will challenge you as obstacles, which in turn will yield your success.

> Sequence Exercise: What is something that has occurred in your past that you had control over and did not like the outcome. What decisions led to that circumstance? What motivated those decisions? Are you currently making decisions with the same motivations? Write these down and determine the path that such decisions may take?

Idealism

"It can be argued that the quickest way an infant learns to speak, move, and even think, is by imitation. They look to their parents, siblings, or anyone else around them as examples." **(YOUNG LEADER)**

C.   <u>I am always learning how to become more successful.</u>

When you find these opportunities, it is imperative that you first know that nothing is truly new. In this book, there is nothing that has not been written or taught elsewhere. So, before you embark on a decision's cause and effect stream, reach out to those who have had similar experiences. This does not mean you should limit yourself to their advice. It means that will increase your ability to navigate the situation if you build upon what they may have to offer. If you are creating a new product or want to embark on a new research project, identify someone who embarked on the same initiative. There are others who have created entirely new areas of study. Read their books, watch their shows, attend their classes, and then decide to do even more effectively and efficiently than they did. This is not recommending that you approach this from a competitive standpoint, but rather as a validating testament to their lives. Because their stories were put to good use. You will be able to prepare yourself for even bigger opportunities because you have safeguarded yourself from some of their obstacles. It is like being ahead of your peers in a class because instead of learning addition when they are learning it, you already know what it means to multiply. Addition may have been taught to you at an age in which you were the most open to learning it. Therefore, you feel no inhibitions when the teacher introduces it.

The other important concept to utilize from this is the idea of idealism. Idealism is not a bad word. Many successful people succeeded by embracing a persistent idealism. This does not mean being unaware or oblivious of the situation in which you are present but finding a way to use the situation to your advantage. There is a story of a woman who really wanted a position at a large company. She did not know how to make her resume stand out, so she sent a shoebox to the person responsible for new hires. The shoebox had one shoe in it with a note. The note read, "Well, since I already have one foot in the door…" She was hired soon after. This technique is not for everyone, but you should be idealistic in how you approach circumstances. "There must be a way that I will discover that thing or accomplish that goal or try that experience." If you have a book and you want to get it published, well then get it published! Find an editor who is seeking your content, and let them know, "I know you are in this business because you enjoy the value that books can bring. Read my book, and I promise you will be encouraged by the value that it brings." Better yet, have someone the editor knows make the recommendation. You will likely be able to get him or her to read the book, but the rest of that interaction is the "systems" part of this scenario. As mentioned before, it is important to understand systems. In contrast to your idealism, understanding these systems represents realism. Your realism should complement your idealism; it should not obstruct it. If your realism overshadows your idealism, you become cynical. People just do not like cynical people, because they serve as a reminder of all the negative consequences of the human emotion of fear. However, because people possess fear as an emotion, too much idealism will make you incredible or incredulous.

Striking a balance between the two will help you when striving toward your goals. You can gauge your balance by how you respond to questions. If someone asks you for advice on a new idea, what is your focus? Are you excited about the possibilities for the idea? Are you listening carefully to determine all the shortcomings? Do you feel worried or insulted? Do you see plans or resources? See below for the traits:

Responses	Realism	Idealism
Reaction	Insulted or nervous	Excited
Advice	Shortcomings and Obstacles	Possibilities and Potential
Next Actions	Create a plan	List of Resources

| Context Used for Advice | Systems at play and Proper Procedures | Standing Out and Shortcuts |

You should possess a mixture of the above characteristics.

III. **I must reflect on my leadership.**

Specular reflection, in engineering terms, is a phenomenon exhibited by light in which the angle the wave is incident on the surface, equals the angle at which it is reflected. The other interesting quality of reflection is that the images are chiral- you cannot superimpose the images on top of each other. How does this translate into leadership development? Well, it means reflections are always going to be a bit skewed but are great when identifying objects behind you. They also indicate when you should change yourself, specifically your appearance, in some way. I am sure before you leave in the morning for class or work that you look into your mirror. You probably make sure your clothes match, and your hair is brushed. If you do not do this every day, hopefully you at least check a mirror before you go on a date or to an interview. After looking in the mirror a few times, you get used to the reversed directions. This is how your reflection on your leadership could work. It will probably be a bit skewed to reality, but you can use it to manage your flaws and prevent something coming from behind and surprising you. Let's dig in, shall we!

> Idealism Exercise: What is the ideal state for your current situation in life, and what obstacles prevent that from being the case? How can you realistically leverage those obstacles to help

you obtain the ideal, whether it be in romance, wealth, health, spirit, or family? Write down a list of all the things you are grateful for that others may not have access to – how can you realistically use those aspects as leverage to achieve your ideal self? Lastly, are you acting, thinking, appearing, or planning the way you would if you were in your ideal state? Are there any changes that you can make? Write these down.

Reflection

"Who is not a companion to his spirit is an enemy to people. And he, who sees not in his self a friend, dies despairing. For life springs from within a man and comes not from without him." **(A Spiritual Treasury)**

    A.   <u>Meditate on my character.</u>

Be deliberate about your reflection through meditation. It should not only be the consequence of someone else asking you to, but it should be self-instructed and consistent. Some forms of meditation involve studying with an object or objective in mind. It implies focus and concentration. You want to consistently study your character. Your character is the compilation of everything that makes up who you are. What are your values? How do you make decisions? What matters the most to you? What motivates you? What is the purpose you dream of and why? If your name were the title of a book, what would your current chapter be and what would the content be in the book? Would others be able to read it? If you take the time to truly understand those aspects of your life, your mirror will become cleaner, and you will be able to navigate yourself. If you know the saying, "you are your worst enemy", part of the meaning and lesson is that you should understand yourself and then be able to predict and manage yourself accordingly.

The consequences of not spending time understanding yourself and figuring out your flaws are the same as going into an interview without checking the mirror. You will be embarrassed, you will appear in a way you never thought you would, and you most likely will not get the job.

In the previous section, it was discussed that there exists a true sequence in the world. You must internalize that your situations are really an expression of how you view your worth. Just like any good investment, it takes time and work to grow. It must be fed new resources and evaluated for progress. If you are performing these tasks, then you will reap the benefits, referencing the quote: *"for life springs from within a man and comes not from without."*

There are many deeds to be done in this world, and you can accomplish the greatest of them, but you are also capable of bringing terror upon others. If you do not understand your breaking points, or your motivations, it will only mean harm to those you love, and people you have never even met.

> Reflection Exercise: Think of someone you know or have heard of that you judge for making bad decisions. Now, imagine yourself making the same bad decisions and what circumstances and emotional states might drive you to that state of mind. Now, reflect on the last time you were happy. How did you act towards others? How did they receive your happiness? Could others tell you were happy? Do the same exercise for sadness, anger, and fear. Were the actions put in the right direction, or did your

emotional state impact other elements in your day? How were other decisions impacted? Did you miss out on any opportunities or make any bad decisions. Now, do the same exercise thinking of the person you judged. Lastly, reflect on what you have learned about yourself. How can you prepare yourself to prevent some emotional states from impacting the rest of your day and or relationships?

Correction

"But not to acknowledge a mistake, not to correct it and learn from it, is a mistake of a different order. It usually puts a person on a self-deceiving, self-justifying path, often involving rationalization (rational lies) to self and to others." **(7 HABITS OF HIGHLY EFFECTIVE PEOPLE)**

    B.   <u>Acknowledge my mistakes.</u>

Take some caution with your actions. You do not have to display your mistakes, but you must acknowledge that things may turn for the worse in any given situation because our world is filled with interacting sequences. Self-righteousness can be easily spotted. If you find yourself saying, "I would never do that" or "how could I ever think that way", you are exhibiting the traits of a self-righteous person. It is great that you have a high regard for yourself; however, the danger is that it is falsely derived. As mentioned before, you are completely capable of an array of deeds. It may take a lot for you to "think that way, or do that thing", but there is a point in which you will. Being self-righteous about it will bear no fruit for you. As a matter of fact, it will lead you down a pathway that will cause you to lie so that you can reinforce your ego.

Practice admitting, at least to yourself, that you were wrong with small things and then work your way up once you are more comfortable. If you have an impulse to pass judgment on another's actions, stop yourself, and wonder why he/she may have committed that action, and determine under which circumstances you could see yourself doing the same. Having this ability is a step into learning how to reflect on your leadership and meditate on your character. It will open a great opportunity to learn from new and familiar situations, and from people who are young and old. It will offer yet another moment of leadership.

> Correction Exercise: Think of a decision you have made recently that has caused grief and stress for others. As we have already discussed the relationship between cause and effect, prudently think of how your decision can be modified to prevent an avalanche of negative consequences. First consider how you can offer atonement. Is it through acknowledgment, listening, extending an olive branch, pressing the reset button, or by some other method? Plan to turn this into action. Then you can use the reset to discover how can the situation be rectified.

Meditation Tenets

A clock always aspires to achieve its next second and thus becomes a clock. It is as such because it is willed and so what it has sought is what it shall be defined until it no longer seeks its next second.

Below are some questions that you should not quickly come to an answer for, but rather find some time to reflect upon. Consider the meaning of these questions (some have multiple meanings), and then meditate on your answers. When you have found your answer, it should feel honest and consistent with who you are.

1. What actions have defined who you are?
2. What are you most prideful about?
3. What mistakes have you tried to ignore?
4. What lessons have you failed to learn?
5. How are you improving?
6. What, if you were a better person, would you do differently? Why?
7. What is something you think you would never do? Why?
8. What in your life is an opportunity for leadership?

Week **Three**

This week's chapter attempts to find a holistic way to describe the world. It involves analysis (separating information to understand the pieces), and synthesis, (reconstructing the pieces into a perspective that you can use to interpret your surroundings). With regards to leadership, it is important to be able to interpret your surroundings to make better decisions. Our thoughts may only go as far as we can understand.

Dimensions of Life

Note: *"Independent thinking alone is not suited to interdependent reality. Independent people who do not have the maturity to think and act interdependently may be good individual producers, but they won't be good leaders or team players. They're not coming from the paradigm of interdependence necessary to succeed in marriage, family, or organizational reality."* **(7 HABITS OF HIGHLY EFFECTIVE PEOPLE)**

When considering how to view your world, it is not suggested to adopt an understanding of the world where you are fully dependent on others. When you enter a situation, you carry with you an order. The sequence of events in your life and the decisions you have made are brought onto every project in which you engage. In this light, you are an independently functioning person. You have thoughts, feelings, skills, inclinations, and relationships that come along with you. When you are hired by a new company, those are the things you bring with you. It is also a fallacy, however, to only consider your independence. As described in the previous chapter, when discussing chaos, your order must interact with the order of others.

This is the basis for the interdependent system that is being referenced in the opening quote. It is not only reality. It must also be your mindset. Even something as simple as attending a class involves decisions made at the national level of the government. Decisions made there affect what resources are available to your school or college. This affects the leadership of your school and influences their decisions. These decisions may result in fires or new hires in the school faculty. Added pressure will affect the performance of your teachers and will influence what you learn in the classroom. An interdependent mentality, however, does not end the story there. As an interdependent person, you can influence the system and not just be influenced by it. You can go to any of the decision points in the system and either change what is available or create new options for what is available. This is what an efficient leader does. The point demonstrated here is the interaction of these orders. This chapter is about the lenses that you can use as evaluative measures for what you want to accomplish, what you think you are accomplishing, and what you are accomplishing.

The operational definition for this chapter is below:

Interdependence is mutual dependence or in the state of depending on each other.

A mentality of dependency limits your ability to influence a situation. It means no one relies on your success, thus you must rely on their good will to care about you. If you make another interested in your success, however, you have created a small interdependent unit. The other individual is now motivated to see you succeed because that success is in their best interest. This is also one of reasons the "joining a team" mentality works. Simply put, if everyone has a vested interest in the positive outcome of a project, they will be more willing to work and put in resources to make sure that it is successful. The workplace environment is evident of such a paradigm. Workers who feel invested in their jobs or projects yield better results than those who are solely functioning off the mechanics of scientific management.

Be aware that this chapter uses mathematical and scientific language to draw corollaries about life. Things to consider about interdependence...

I. **Think in four dimensions of life.**

The best way to comprehend the point in this chapter is to think of the dimensions as parameters. Parameters are characteristics that are unique and independent but can be arranged in a way, notably applied in mathematics, to demonstrate relationships or create models. The results of the model are affected by the prescribed parameters. For a square, the model of its area considers the parameter of the length of a side. For the volume of a tire, however, multiple radii and cross-sectional area are taken into consideration.

The important concept is that models are meant to describe or predict an entity and parameters are used to create models. This chapter is meant to model life, and the parameters are what this book is deeming as the four dimensions. It is important to consider all the parameters and to that end they are analyzed independently of each other. However, if life presents a change, then each of the parameters are also changing. Each parameter's interdependence is demonstrated with every change you experience.

Another important idea to consider is the utility and purpose of creating and applying models. Models allow for the opportunity to evaluate and estimate results. This is important because with models, you can make better decisions. The closer a model is to reality, the less un-factored uncertainty is present. This concept of uncertainty and parameter choice also goes into the complexity of the model that is being created. There are some parameters that are perhaps impossible to obtain: Heisenberg's Uncertainty Principle discusses just one aspect in the mechanics of subatomic particles. So, the more high-level the parameters become, the more useful they are, but the trade-off is that they are harder to configure, and the model becomes less reliable. If there were to be a disavowal of the proposed dimensions of life, it would be due to the complexity involved in each of the parameters reviewed below.

Accessibility

"As an interdependent person, I have the opportunity to share myself deeply, meaningfully, with others, and I have access to the vast resources and potential of other human beings." **(A SPIRITUAL TREASURY)**

      A.   <u>The Social Dimension allows for collective groups to operate for the greater good. It is the outside perception.</u>

Normally, there are three dimensions that are presented in philosophical books. One that is, however, frequently left out is the dimension that involves shared interactions. It is everything that is a part of the cause-and-effect interplay of systems. A fruit is known to be good based upon how it interacts with a person. Eating fruit is, however, the product of many processes that must occur. A fruit is the bearing of a plant, and the plant is said to provide a fruit as its benefit to the world. When discovering your social parameters, your fruits are the products of many internal processes with which others do not engage. It is in the Social Dimension of your life that others can gain meaning from you. If you only want to share weak fruit, then it is your decision to do so. That will be all that is shared. If you choose to share or produce plenty of fruit, then the world will eat of it. Their judgments will be based on their experience with your fruit: its taste and its nutritional value.

Purpose and value are expressed in the Social Dimension. Imagine book that cannot be read by anyone. What value might it possess if there is no hope that it may ever be read? Life can be evaluated based upon the value that a certain action or object provides. When you evaluate yourself in this light, you can see the benefit and harm that you bring to others and can adjust accordingly. Groups can make functional decisions from doing a "Social Dimension" evaluation. It works by using the sum of the parts and their interactions with other entities. In business, transactions occur amongst multiple parties. Strategy, organization, marketing, financing, and management decisions all can be made by looking at the interactions between the company and its customers.

For an individual, this translates into determining your perceived value. How do others feel around you? What do you give others? What do you do for others? What do people do for you? Why do people treat you the way they do? The last question is very important to consider. Any time you interact with someone, they can only make judgments from what you share about yourself. Your words and actions may be very revealing and allow others to make even more significant discoveries about you. Others then relate what you present to their own experiences and consequently create expectations. So, if you are being treated in a certain way, try to understand what you are conveying. It is here that perceptions are created. When considering your communication, perceptions are just as valid as truths. They come from two places: predominant perceptions and convicted perceptions. Predominant perceptions are the easiest to alter. They are derived primarily because of fads or phases. They are adopted to "fit-in". Convicted perceptions are, however, tied into the ego of the individual who possesses them. The ego can be offended or exalted. You should be aware of the ramifications for what you say and what you do in the Social Dimension.

> Accessibility Exercise: What is your external brand? How do others think of you and what benefits do they derive? How do others access you? These answers will differ by relationship type. By listening, you can determine how you are seen. Make a list of which relationships see you in which way: A savior, a diplomat, a provider, a creator, a star/perfect, an organizer, an obligation, a therapist, a motivator, an accomplishment, or a refuge. Once you are clear on how you are seen and under which circumstances, you can understand how you move in the Social Dimension.

Calculation

"Lead them into the moment- an intensified present in which morality, judgment, and concern for the future all melt away and the body succumbs to pleasure." **(ART OF SEDUCTION)**

> B. <u>The Physical Dimension describes your sensory perceptions. It is what you do.</u>

The Physical Dimension is all about existence. That a thing exists and can be described is a part of the Physical Dimension. It is the object or person with which you interact. It is void of the interactions that may exist between the thing and another. All perceptions can be altered, at least temporarily, by changing the Physical Dimension. Evaluation in this dimension does not rely on the interaction of the object but singularly on its existence. A plant that bears fruit is simply a plant that bears fruit. Favoring, eating, and digesting the fruit would fit into the Social Dimension for that plant. The fruit you bear may not benefit anyone. Thus, its value is rendered useless. Still, it does not mean that you have not created fruit. In business, the Physical Dimension consists of office space, office items, properly filed paperwork, and a product. Decisions regarding personal preferences and structure can be made based on evaluations in the Physical Dimension.

Your talents would be described in the Physical Dimension. You sing, dance, write, create, speak, swim, workout, walk, run, and the list can go on. The Social Dimension determines the perceived value, however. The Physical Dimension determines what is being valued. These talents can be noticed by simply paying attention to your most common conversations. If the relationship between the Social and the Physical are that the Social dictates value and the Physical presents the entity to be valued, then when you are interacting, the things you present are a part of the Physical.

Just as others can pass judgments, you are also able to do so. You can use this to your advantage by taking your Physical Dimension attributes and passing judgments on them. Try to imagine yourself from the outside and dictate your value to yourself. What do you commend yourself on, and what do you denigrate? The Physical Dimension evaluation can give you a window into your own perceptions and prepare you to not only calculate an appropriate reaction or initiation, but to also prepare for the reactions and initiations of others.

> Calculation Exercise: Make a list of your skills and talents. Determine which ones you would like to introduce to the Social Dimension.

Motivation

"The Seed. The soil is carefully prepared. The seeds are planted months in advance. Once they are in the ground, no one knows what hand threw them there. Disguise your manipulations by planting seeds that take root on their own." **(ART OF SEDUCTION)**

    C.   <u>The Mental Dimension is a very powerful dimension which to be in one accord. It describes your intelligence and "how" you do.</u>

The Mental Dimension is more conceptual in nature. It involves the uncontrolled inner workings of a particular entity. It is the design of the product. To continue the analogy of the fruit bearing plant, the Mental Dimension would be the kind of seed that was initially planted. A sunflower seed may never become a rose. Therefore, it should not attempt to be a rose, but to be a sunflower that bears the physical attributes of a sunflower. The Mental Dimension can be crafted by your genetic material or by behavioral instructions exercised by your guardians. When evaluating in this dimension, it is important to realize what influences you. Perhaps it is your region of birth, sex, or age. The Mental Dimension is the sum of all those influences. It is here where you can grasp that you can devise strategic plans to either cause harm or benefit. You can determine what motivates you and what limits you. The Mental Dimension evaluation is very complex. It involves understanding your thoughts and desires. For you, at what point do consequences offer less risk than a potential reward?

Some products of philosophy also include the Emotional Dimension, yielding a 5-tier method by which you may analyze the world. This book, however, has consolidated the Emotional Dimension to exist within the Mental Dimension as they are inextricably tied to one another. Your ability to reason and be intelligent is directly influenced by your desires. It can be analyzed using the same methods of the Mental Dimension, but emotions themselves are objects influenced by the four dimensions outlined in this chapter. As mentioned in the beginning of this chapter, there are many ways to view the world, and the proposition of four dimensions is simply one of them.

By understanding and evaluating this parameter of life, you can predict the involvement and motivations of others. Thus, when one mentions the idea of planting a seed, they mean that they are influencing another's views of their design or motivations for their decisions. While perceptions may be influenced in the Physical Dimension quite easily, altering the Mental Dimension can be devastating for an individual. Diversions in this dimension are much harder to craft and involve a deep understanding of how emotional systems operate. The things you fear, love, and hope for are all blueprinted into this dimension. When communicating in this realm, you are maneuvering in the Mental Dimension. How you view yourself here (Mental Dimension) affects how you display yourself (Physical Dimension), and how others interact with you (Social Dimension). If you are willing to take the time to comprehend this parameter, you can begin a process of behavioral reprogramming.

In business, vision and mission statements are a part of the Mental Dimension. The vision and mission statements often vividly express what the company believes is qualitatively worth and capable of achieving. Every operating decision you make should be to accomplish the vision/ mission. These statements are the fundamental beliefs of the promise that the business holds. Clearly, if the Mental Dimension is so fundamental to the many decisions businesses make, so is the dimension also pivotal to the decisions you make about yourself.

When referencing "how" you do, the statement offers a method for identifying the mechanism that is the Mental Dimension. To begin identifying what the Mental Dimension consists of, think of how you interact and the influences that drive those interactions. Is it that you may be afraid of loneliness? Perhaps you are afraid of rejection. Beginning with your fears, hopes, and loves will assist in discovering your Mental Dimension and begin to evaluate it so that you may make better decisions. Once you identify your motivations, you have the option to change them. *How* you believe something can be changed by understanding *why* you believe something.

Intelligence is referencing how your experiences play into your understanding. Knowledge obtained through other people, books, or experiences all can be incorporated into intelligence. Your ability to recognize patterns and make predictions based off those patterns is crucial to your survival. The Mental Dimension is not concerned with why you must survive, but it does believe that it must, and is left to determine how.

> Motivation Exercise: Revisit your list of talents and skills from the previous exercise and add an explanation for why you want to bring the talents you selected to the Social Dimension.

Depth of Why

"Faith is a knowledge within the heart, beyond the reach of proof."
(A SPIRITUAL TREASURY)

D. <u>The Spiritual Dimension has the greatest importance and influence. It describes your intellect. It explains "why".</u>

Keep asking yourself why. What is the deeper meaning? What makes people care? Think of the entire universe. Picture each of the planets and the stars and asteroids that surround them. Imagine how dark it is. Picture the sun. Picture the Earth, which is like a marble to a basketball. Imagine yourself on the surface of the Earth in your little room with a ceiling reading this extremely small book. Think of the vast oceans and never-ending sky with seven billion people carrying on conversations, eating, sleeping, dying, laughing, and playing. Imagine the many people that have come and gone on this planet and the lives they led. Replay the wars, the pandemics, the meteorological catastrophes, and the worldwide aid missions. Imagine the changes in technology: transportation, communication, and health. The world is vast.

Every system is arbitrary. They are explained and proven by metrics. "One" has a meaning because it has been dictated. In learning mathematics, you can progress from addition to multiplication, and then to exponents. The building blocks for each step are based in a successful adoption of assumptions as you progress higher. If any of the assumptions were to change, the entire system would be compromised. In engineering, axioms, postulates, and laws can be used and not broken. We accept that magnetism, electricity, and gravity, are all in existence and an engineer could manipulate them. They do not have to be fully understood to accomplish something with them. However, the greater the understanding, the more configuration is afforded. In every aspect of our lives, we display a phenomenon known as faith. Whether it is in a higher being or in our own perceptions, we want to believe that there is truth in something. As mentioned in the standards of leadership, a leader understands that there is truth in everything.

Our biggest truth is in the concept of existence. As a child, you may have questioned, what if I am the only one that is alive, and all other entities are products of my imagination. You quickly learn that it cannot be the case unless our minds are able to create, configure, and separate new entities. If you could create your world, you would be able to predict it. Nevertheless, there is a link between you and other entities. This link affords you some predictability. Evolutionarily speaking, you can speak and ask questions so that you may understand and predict others. You play mind games to realize the motivations of others and look for windows to comprehend their options when given false decisions. You rely on a system when you participate in these mind games. The system is the most basic assumption that you can make in your setting and allows you to configure survival and need obtainment. Your reliance on the system is faith. Albeit a god, God, or consequence of science, you faithfully rely on the system to work each time.

When you walk, eat, sleep, work, and play, you rely on the system. In general, we are attracted to religion because it offers us a deeper understanding beyond the Mental Dimension. It is the Spiritual Dimension. In this dimension, your primal beliefs simmer and determine everything about who you are and what you do subconsciously and unconsciously. The system had to come from somewhere. In the fruit metaphor, the Spiritual Dimension is the planting of the seed. There was intention in the planting and in the design. The seed cannot change but by influence. Had it never been planted, there would be no sunflowers.

In business, there is confidence that the business system exists and that the core assumption is true: if you provide for a need, people will take it. How it happens is up to the design, the product, and how the business interacts. However, the assumption that people will take what they need or that people must survive is just that, an assumption. Such an assumption may or may not always be the case. As for the world we live in, it is. It tends to work out that when people are compelled to buy, they buy. When they are left with a choice to live or die, they usually choose to live.

Intellect implies a sense of intuition in addition to your intelligence. Intuition is much more mysterious. It can be explained as an intelligent response that is the result of understanding the flow and position of the operating systems. In which systems do you possess faith? What assumptions have you made about them and their existence? *"Why do people want to survive"* is a basic question. A corresponding question might be, *"What is my purpose?"* This is the hardest dimension to alter. However, when this realm is understood and changed, it has the greatest impact. If you find yourself in repeat situations that you do not want, you should refer to your Spiritual Dimension. There is perhaps something you believe about yourself that you do not want to believe. The surfacing perception, however, will be the one that is controlling your subconscious and your unconscious in addition to your conscious.

Something as simple as shyness or obesity usually takes residence in the Spiritual realm. Your shyness may come from your belief that you have nothing important to say. It is important to be honest because this realm only recognizes honesty. It can distinguish when you are providing falsities. Determine what you believe because you will receive exactly what you want.

II. **These dimensions are interdependent. They are interlaced and stacked, and each has its cause and its effect.**

Unlike mathematics, where parameters are truly independent of one another, in life, these parameters are interdependent. These dimensions are considered focuses. You can focus on evaluating yourself in any of the four. The latter requires the most effort, but the former offers the greatest tangible risks/ rewards for a short amount of time. Your focuses will determine how people treat you, how you treat others, and how well you are able to predict yourself and others. Unknowing masters of these evaluations became some of the World's Greats. They play the world like a chess game. They all fall to some inevitability or vice, however, and it would be wise for you to understand the perceptions: what, how, and why. Perhaps your fall may be prevented if you do.

Keep in mind that the Spiritual realm influences the Mental which in turn influences the Physical. The Physical then influences the Social, and from that, you may construct the world we live in. Our focuses and orders meld together to create our systems. These systems, in turn, may be influenced by our focuses and orders. If you can control multiple orders, you then can create your own system.

> Depth of Why Exercise: Reflect on what is unique about this day and time that the skills and talents you selected are important to others. Even beyond your personal motivations, what could be the motivation of all things for your existence? How does it fit into the larger context of the world and the future? Is it promoting your concept of goodness? Is it defending against your concept of evil? Are you in a repeated situation -- what lesson is your life continuously teaching you?

Function

"You will kindly remember, however, that the Three Great Planes are not actual divisions of the Universe, but merely arbitrary terms

used by the Hermeticists in order to aid in the thought and study of the various degrees and forms of universal activity and life" **(KYBALION)**

    A.   <u>They describe your leadership.</u>

The quote references three dimensions: the Spiritual, the Mental and the Physical. Recall that there are many ways to evaluate life both qualitatively and quantitatively. The proposition of these four dimensions is another arbitrary method of doing so. Every complex problem and simple object can be analyzed and reconfigured to some degree by the application of the proposed dimensions. By using them to describe your leadership, you can better define the kind of leader you want to be and be better able to discern and engage in opportunities. Each dimension acts as a filter for both your experiences and communication.

Your leadership in the Social Dimension is what you will be known for, since it is the social facet that interacts with others. When you think of great leaders, you dwell on the effects of their accomplishments. These accomplishments are the manifestations of the subconscious and the unconscious aspects of those leaders.

In the Physical Dimension, you think of what they did, void of value or reason or rhyme. You think of their organization and calculated moves. Conquering lands, changing legislation, building a school, filing a paper, designing an airplane, cleaning a room, raising a child, and even buying an item are all considered actions or completed tasks. These things are attributed values once moved into the Social Dimension.

In the Mental Dimension, you think of their influencing motivations and their underlying character. How did they achieve their accomplishments? Was it with sternness? Did they do it with luck or confidence? Were they conceited? Did they feel entitled to their accomplishments? These emotional states of existence become actions and reactions when moved into the Physical Dimension.

Finally, in the Spiritual Dimension, you wonder, what was the reason for them being put into the system? What craftiness went into the design? Did they understand a certain goodness or evilness to their deeds? What makes them different from another person? These fundamental beliefs, morals, values, become emotional expectations in the Mental Dimension.

Thus, you should reflect on yourself in the same capacity. Run evaluations of yourself in all the dimensions to create a full picture of who you are, and what it means to think of yourself as a leader.

As a reminder, you are always a leader because you are always making decisions and are accountable for those decisions. Even a decision to do nothing or keep quiet is still a decision. Be aware of your leadership.

> Function Exercise: Think about how you have led your life? How would others describe it?

Meditation Tenets
A frame itself does not know its content, and the observer may perceive its beauty in fullness. However, the framer has the complete

and magnificent power to determine its content – the framer must simply choose.

Below are some questions that you should not quickly come to an answer for, but rather find some time to reflect upon. Consider the meaning of these questions (some have multiple meanings), and then meditate on your answers. When you have found your answer, it should feel honest and consistent with who you are.

1. How do you perceive the world?
2. In which dimension do you primarily spend time understanding yourself?
3. Why do you spend most of your time there?
4. Would you like to keep spending your time in that dimension? Why?
5. How would you describe your leadership in each dimension? How do people receive your leadership? What do you do to make decisions? What motivates those decisions and how do you rationalize your decisions? How are you wired and what perspectives are a part of your rationalization? How do you know you are on track?
6. Where do emotions exist in this dimensional framework? Why?
7. In which dimension do you think you communicate with others?
8. How familiar are you with your framework?

Week **Four**

The purpose of this week's chapter is to determine what a good decision looks like with regards to short and long-term consequences. The win-win mentality option views compromise as a fallback plan and seeks methods to achieve everyone's objectives. It can be an indirect pathway to becoming a leader of respect and admiration. You can be a leader who changes position at the publics' interest or personal whim; but to be the greatest leader, it takes something of a different essence – it is the ability to create new and inclusive options.

Win-Win Mentality

Note: "The Principle of Win/Win is fundamental to success in all our interactions and embraces five interdependent dimensions of life. It begins with character, and moves toward relationships, but of which flow agreements. It is nurtured in an environment where structure and systems are based on win/win mentality. And it involves process; we cannot achieve win/win end with win/lose or lose/win means." (7 Habits of Highly Effective People)

Whenever something happens in life, you are given the chance to respond or react. The primary difference is that a reaction is an action whereas a response is communicated through multiple formats. A response also carries with it a definition that infers an action or statement was "thought out". Naturally, when confronted with an obstacle, we try to move it or ourselves out of the way. We rarely think of that obstacle as an opportunity for collaboration. The win-win mentality is not a natural reaction and takes practice to achieve it as a default response. Choosing that you would rather respond than react means you must see every scenario and obstacle as an opportunity to plan.

When presented with an opportunity to plan, there is a certain mentality you must possess. Much of what has been discussed has been about understanding your surroundings by reflecting on your perceptions. Taking one step further, the win-win mentality is about understanding your options. At any given time in a relationship or situation, you are presented with a multitude of options: false options, unpleasant options, and desirable options. All the options are analyzed based on the benefit/harm analysis that they provide to you. However, you can create options that provide even more desirable results than the ones that are usually presented. This chapter focuses on training your mind to be in the habit of deriving its own options that are desirable, that maintain true to your standards as explored in the prior chapter.

What are the benefits of the win-win mentality? Firstly, you will establish an environment of trust and loyalty. Since you are thinking of the needs and motivations of others, they will also perceive that you are highly concerned with their well-being in addition to your own. So, even when you are not able to deliver satisfactory results, they will suppose it was the best option possible because they were participants in deriving the options. In leadership, or decision making, loyalty and trust are the currency of effectiveness. Many revolutionary changes can occur over long periods of time, but the benefits of the specific plan or goal you may be trying to implement may be compromised by the impediments that arise within the short term. Most people can agree on a vision, but it takes a lot of work to get people to agree on the details. So, building trust and loyalty can afford you time and acceptance so that your "revolutionary" changes are possible and sustainable.

The other benefit to practicing a win-win mentality is maneuverability. When a win-win mentality is employed, the playing field for strategy becomes more ordered. By anticipating moves (the reactions and actions of others), you can prepare for multiple outcomes and heighten your ability to maneuver around obstacles. You practice this when you have mentors who give you advice. They receive benefits of validation from the relationship they have with you. You receive their resources. When they provide and you consider the caveats of certain activities, you are practicing a planning mentality. You can plan your preparation and anticipate your weaknesses and how they may be used to hurt or help you. Win-win helps because it requires you to plan and stay focused on what is important. This chapter argues that approaching problems with the motivation of seeking a win-win solution will return the most benefit for all parties involved.

The operational definition for this chapter is below:

"Mentality" is a word to describe someone's outlook on life, or more importantly, their intellectual capabilities or endowment.

Things to consider about your mentality...

I. **Practice the Win-Win Mentality.**

To practice something, you must understand what it is. As aforementioned, a mentality is an outlook. It is a manner of thinking and originates from your mental dimension, as described in the previous chapter. "Mentality" describes a manner of information processing or general approach to information. While information may vary in size, content, or meaning, the way we process the information has a significant effect on our lives and our decision-making capabilities. Your mentality should be something that you develop and continuously evaluate to check your perspective and adjust your perceptions. Win-win connotes the positive emotions associated with success or victory. Approaching a situation with the win-win combination requires that firstly, a relationship exists and secondly that all parties in the relationship are gaining a triumphant success or victory. Future chapters focus on the Theory of Abundance, which is the basis of practicing a win-win approach.

There are other forms of mentalities you may possess. Most people function in lose/win, win/lose mentalities. These kinds of mentalities have been ingrained in our brains, perhaps by evolutionary design. Zero-sum game theory plays to validate these thinkers. In a nutshell, it means that if someone wins, then there must be a loser. In competition, business or in athletics, if someone wins a game or a customer, then a competitor loses the game or the customer. This is the simplest of all mentalities you may possess. It is a performance-heavy mentality. The options to win or to lose are present and one or the other will happen regardless of what you do or how you prepare. In a basketball game, the players on both teams have put in a tireless number of hours to improving their skills and studying the plays and skills of their opponent. However, there is no consistent way to predict who will win the game and who will lose the game. There are multi-million-dollar industries that thrive on this type of uncertainty. As a matter of fact, no effort is really put into the planning stage. Performance is planned, but the systems coordinating the game are not objects of the plan. While planning may increase your odds of winning, planning is not a prerequisite to participate in the game.

Lose/lose mentality is much rarer and can be found in populations of those who feel sorrow and want to spread their sorrow. "If I do not win, then no one will win." These mentalities are dangerous and self-destructive. Competition can at least be friendly. In lose/lose, you will not only lose your opportunities, but you will lose your relationships and any credibility you had will be written off as a lie. Lose/lose players are always victims and search for more victims to add to their inventory. Avoid having this mentality and being influenced by those who possess it. If a person uses this mentality to process information, they will find happiness fleeting, and you can do nothing to help them as they find comfort in the consistency of being a victim. This complacency is a byproduct of our need to make things predictable. Note that predictability is important for survival and allows us to make decisions. If nothing exhibited causality or predictability, we would find ourselves in a state of constant fear and paranoia.

Win-win is planning-heavy. It requires that you have identified options, players, and key factors. You then must stage your subsequent actions and decisions so that you can gain an outcome that benefits all participants. This mentality cannot be employed without planning and understanding what other factors are involved. If the planning is not completed, then the mentality falls back into the win/lose, lose/win because there will be someone's need that is not being met.

Finally, what is practice? Practicing involves consistent and deliberate engagement of some tool or activity. Practicing a mentality can qualify as both. So, as we continue throughout this chapter, I encourage you to think of the scenarios in your life that trouble you. Think of one to use as we go through the steps of practicing the win-win mentality.

Consideration

"Instead of looking for the best alternative for the long term, people who are defensive lose the ability to get past their own involvement." **(YOUNG LEADER)**

    A. It makes us more creative.

Win-win mentality is a planning-heavy mentality. It requires that several orders are explored (an order is a series of cause-and-effect relationships). The emotional orders of the individuals, the orders of the systems at play, and the order of their changes over time should be the variables at the top of the list. There will always be unconsidered factors, but the more you can safeguard against uncontrollable factors, the better the result will be. This approach is evident in the Scientific Method where variables (factors of potential influence) are controlled in the attempt to apply a consistent measure. However, when a difficult problem has many degrees of freedom, it is upon the solver or the mathematician to creatively devise assumptions. In a transport system, those assumptions may be with regards to shape, area, flux, time, or some other parameter. The goal of these assumptions is to do two things: decrease the number of unknowns and synthesize equations to mathematically model the process. The same happens with a win-win mentality's approach to problem solving.

Considering the factors does not mean to simply acknowledge their existence, but to be able to parameterize it enough so that the unknown factors will not apply or are, at best, approximated. This kind of problem solving involves a high amount of creativity. How well do you develop options and models that were not originally given in the presented problem? This approach involves thinking outside of the box.

It takes a change in perspective. When looking at problems, there are a few ways to achieve viewing through another lens without having to reevaluate your belief system. However, many times our beliefs are the psychologically inherent obstacles that cause us to not interpret a problem in a more robust manner.

So, step one involves listening to the other parties before a situation arises. Speaking to others will help to provide insight from other angles. Asking questions that require open-ended answers will help in discovering factors that may not have even been considered. Consider the opinions, experiences, and motivations of others. Are they motivated by family, wealth, legacy, experiences, validation, or accomplishment? Are they inspired by others, or do they derive energy from within? How do they approach decisions and plans? Are they meticulous and regimented? Are they open-minded? Are they agreeable? Are they still trying to prove themselves? By just listening to someone, you can learn plenty that can then be incorporated into the win-win plan. Not being able to imagine beyond your own involvement in a ploy, plan, or project, will limit your ability to make appropriate risk-taking decisions with the available resources.

Reflection on long-term cause and effect relationships is also imperative for practicing win-win mentality. You must develop a sixth sense for changing tides. You should reflect on the mentality of those around you. Otherwise, they will create obstructions that you will not see coming. Perhaps they are intimidated by you or are unconvinced of your ability to persevere. Either way, by ignoring their mentalities and how they will come into play as you gain accolades will bring about your own ruin. Over time, people, places, and circumstances change. Sometimes, they change abruptly. In your creativity, do not simply solve your immediate problem, but try to frame it in the context of an even larger problem. There, your solution will have a greater impact. In economic policy, for instance, it may be great to increase subsidies on a commodity, but over the long-term, it may cause more havoc if one does not consider the relationship between supply and demand or regressive taxes. If the subsidy cannot be sustained or does not eventually effectuate a transition to a sustainable remedy, then the effort might only be appropriate in the short-term.

> Consideration Exercise: In the next conversation you have, spend time listening to the person you are with? What are they communicating? Why are they communicating? What message are they trying to convey? Why are they trying to convey that message? What tools and words are they using to accomplish that goal? Then, when you go home, make a note of what you have learned about that individual. Also, if you are networking and someone gives you a business card, get in the habit of writing something you've learned about the individual on the card.

Results

"A relationship where bank accounts are high and both parties are deeply committed to Win/Win is the ideal springboard for tremendous energy. That relationship neither makes the issues any less real or important, nor eliminates the differences in perspective. But it does eliminate the negative energy..." **(7 HABITS OF HIGHLY EFFECTIVE PEOPLE)**

B. <u>We obtain the most positive results.</u>

The bank account referenced is not one that holds physical currency, but rather an account that exists between you and every person with which you have a relationship. It is the emotional account you open when you first meet someone. The first impression is the initial deposit, and the value of that account goes up and down depending on the interactions that follow. The last chapter stressed the importance of relationships for understanding. If others are to trust that you have their best interest in mind, then it's also important to continuously invest in that relationship to keep the account positive.

Win-win is planning-heavy and results-focused. Who benefits? How many people benefit? How many people are harmed and how can you prevent their harm? The kind of options you create should be positive. If there are loose ends, keep trying to tie them up. When you can no longer find a losing party, you have reached your maximum creativity. The options created are then evaluated for their overall benefit. While it is impossible to always make everyone happy, this mentality will allow you to achieve the most positive results. One of the fastest ways to derail a win-win is to have a win-lose mentality on the team. The win-lose mentality requires much less work or if it requires equivalent work, is meant for the demise of another party. Either way neither provides good business or personal karma, and efforts should be made as a leader to mitigate the influence of that individual's win-lose mentality.

The created options should be positive.

As an individual: Be sure to balance your idealism and realism as aforementioned and begin to move forward with a plan. You should constantly reflect on it and develop it as it should be flexible. Your options should benefit you on multiple levels and those that may be affected by your decision.

In a group: Once you cannot creatively configure new and usable parameters, introduce your idea or plan to the group. Anticipate your group's reactions to your idea. You should be flexible in your presentation so that everyone may perceive a certain amount of buy-in, as explained by the "join the team" strategy of presenting ideas. Keep in mind that you are aiming for the best possible option, and the participation of the rest of your team will be necessary to create it.

> Results Exercise: What is something you are attempting to achieve but are encountering obstruction? Find a way to articulate it succinctly. What do your selected words mean to your target audience?

Reputation

"Seeking to understand requires consideration; seeking to be understood takes courage. Win/Win Mentality requires a high degree of both." **(7 HABITS OF HIGHLY EFFECTIVE PEOPLE)**

    C. <u>We will always approach circumstances in this way.</u>

When a person engages in an activity on a consistent basis, it begins to develop that person's reputation. Your reputation is directly tied to your actions and the expectations of others. It is indirectly influenced and altered by others by which you have no control. The reason to always approach circumstances in this manner is to accomplish a few objectives.

1)   Practice

By practicing this mentality with small endeavors or decisions, it will become a habit. Never appear to be indecisive, however, as it will encourage fear in anyone who chooses to follow you, including yourself. The time it takes to consider options and devise new ones should be perceived as the application of diligence and intelligence and not uncertainty. Imagine a man who quickly and wittingly can create a solution to a problem that many others have attempted to solve. He will be regarded highly for his astuteness and gain loyalty. The practice will allow you to develop that mentality and apply it more effectively and efficiently so that it may be put to good use. You will be able to anticipate the perceptions and actions of others due to your new multilateral way of seeing a problem. Think: a pyramid appears to be a square or a triangle when viewed from one angle.

2) Results

Creative and positive results are desirable results. Creative means original and in business where originality becomes a competitive advantage, creativity can be good. "Positive results" are results that are beneficial. In finance, business, policy, entertainment, information management, accounting, engineering, research, and every other professional category, positive results are a necessity.

3) Reputation

In the Social Dimension, a reputation can be liquid. It can be used to hurt others, help yourself, or harm yourself, in the case of extortion, and to help others, as does an endorsement. Your reputation can help chart your route to your dream. Reputation, as aforementioned, is directly influenced by your actions and your expectations. Win-win mentality will build your reputation as someone who is trustworthy, progressive, and diligent. Refer to the table below to see which adjectives may become associated to your leadership because of your mentality.

Win-Win	Win-Lose	Lose-Win	Lose-Lose
Diligent	Stern	Pessimistic	Vindicated
Loyal	Intelligent	Useless	Rationalizing
Intelligent	Loyal	Sacrificial	Useless
Trusting Followers	Competitive	Competitive	Risky
Progressive	Callous	Pawn-like	Dangerous

For the win-lose relationship, this type of individual is mostly concerned with the best outcome for himself. At the pinnacle of practicing win-lose mentality, you will become great at what you do and accumulate much success throughout your life. Since you have become obedient to your trade and made decisions accordingly, you will appear with a certain amount of sternness and intelligence. Others will commend your ability to serve yourself in an outstanding manner.

At the same time, however, others will assume you do not have their best interest at heart and will deny them an opportunity if there is the perception that it will threaten your success. In this way, the followers of a win-lose personality will go to great lengths to prove that they can be trusted by such a leader. They are, however, functioning out of fear that they may be forced to become a competitor. So, they usually live dual lives of outwardly supporting you and secretly trying to identify a way to move you out of power and enforce their own practice of win-lose. They will spurn you once you lose power as they always secretly believed you were self-serving and callous.

A lose-win relationship is a relationship in which the individual is self-sacrificing for the benefit of others. While this may seem a noble approach, understand that the individual who is self-sacrificing also has individuals who rely on their success. Others who watch a person functioning with this mentality will be forced to play on the individual's weaknesses. This kind of mentality is usually justified with a sense of self-righteousness and rooted in an interpretation of philosophical or religious piety. These deep-seeded beliefs can easily be used against a person because it allows for a certain amount of predictability. When someone is predictable, they can be forced to take options. A win-lose mentality will use another's lose-win mentality to achieve its objectives. It is only useful to be on the competitor's side of a person practicing the lose-win mentality. Playing on this person's team in which your individual needs are not met will yield a fruitless relationship. You cannot truly grow.

Another caveat of the lose-win relationship is one in which the individual becomes so consumed by his own self-righteousness and lack of success, that he or she becomes a pessimist- that nothing beneficial for them should come out of their deeds. Deliberate self-sacrifice will scare others and will make you an obvious pawn.

Finally, the lose-lose mentality is the mentality of "If I cannot have it, then no one can". This leadership type is purely one of a movement. It can be extremely powerful, but dangerous. Working towards the demise of others in lieu of your failure is extremely motivating but will lead to the most extreme set of adjectives of all adjectives in the Social Dimension. This type makes excuses and rationalizes everything without accommodating the investments of others (many times the investments are considered, but in the context of destroying them). Many individuals will see these types as useless as they provide no beneficial value in the Social Dimension and are extremely risky. They are much harder to predict since as a collective, people usually do not reflect on the opinions and methods of "evil doers". We focus on the mentalities of those who do well and do good deeds. Understanding the ability to do "evil" will allow a win-win mentality to master a lose-lose mentality.

Every situation is truly unique and may provide temptations to revert to another mentality. You must know who you are dealing with. The lesson of this chapter is to express the opinion that the win-win mentality will provide the greatest benefit and will assist you in doing the most with your skill set and personality.

II. It requires a relationship.

Properly practicing a win-win mentality requires a few ingredients. What is a relationship? A relationship is an agreement between two or more parties to participate in some accordance with each other. The agreement may be implied or explicit. Relationships go awry when one party does not realize they are in a relationship nor understand the terms of the relationship. Relationships are important to reflect on: they consist of individuals with different interests, experiences, expectations, and orders. When two people are trying to establish a relationship, both parties begin with familiar territory. Conversations usually border along a brief description of a day and perhaps the weather. Someone then decides to take a leap of faith on a similar interest based on the detail of the brief description of the day. Over time, each person begins to identify with and anticipate the other person. This is where the win-win mentality begins.

> Reputation Exercise: Who is someone you know that uses the Win-Win Mentality? What is their brand? Which of your relationships need repair?

Discussion

"Win/Win Mentality is not a belief in the Third Alternative. It's not your way or my way; it it's a better way, a higher way." **(7 HABITS OF HIGHLY EFFECTIVE PEOPLE)**

A. <u>All parties must be understood.</u>

In the case of beginning a relationship, each person's interests must be determined. For a win-win game to be played, the objectives should be explicit. Otherwise, there will be parties who will not have their expectations met. This kind of accord is developed through open discussion. All concerns can be voiced and explored. The goal should be for everyone to voice their "vision". The details can be configured and pieced together. For discussion, there should be a main objective to achieve. There are some cautions with discussion:

1) Problem-solving can become ineffective or inefficient if an effective timekeeper and notetaker are not in place.
2) Emotions will run high if there is a disagreement in approaching a problem, so maintaining focus on a meeting objective is necessary.
3) There will be a mixture of games being played (win-win, win-lose, lose-win, lose-lose) during a discussion, so maintaining a t-chart on benefits and pitfalls will help to keep the group thinking more creatively.
4) Everyone will not explicitly state their interests or objectives, so encourage the group to provide their opinion on specific ideas by asking compare and contrast questions for presented ideas.
5) Strong personalities and power holders will influence the explicitness of the opinions of weaker personalities and subordinates. So, approaching the strong personality first to win them over should work in your favor. The other line of approach includes approaching the other members first,

but you will risk ostracizing the strong personality and further create a dichotomy in a group. The approach can be intentional or inadvertent. Either way, you should be prepared for the recoil.

In discussion, however, everyone is simultaneously going into an agreement, and setting objectives so that a plan of action may ensue. In win-win mentality, the solution is not a compromise solution. The solution is very methodical and anticipatory. Much of the planning will be done individually, but the objectives should be clear in the context of the discussion. Everyone should be able to propose options and then the final decision should be a combination of many reflections and considerations so that the desired results may be obtained.

> Discussion Exercise: Write down how you could improve an upcoming meeting you have where you can create a more win-win environment.

Comprehension

"...Seek first to understand, then to be understood. This principle is a key to effective interpersonal communication" **(7 HABITS OF HIGHLY EFFECTIVE PEOPLE)**

B. <u>Understand "why" a party wants something and not just "what" they want.</u>

There are two important components of comprehension: passive sensing and active sensing.

Close your eyes and try to be silent. You will begin to hear many sounds in your surroundings. You may hear others having conversations, perhaps a television or video game, the humming of the refrigerator, or even of the electricity going through the wires in a light bulb. You may hear your heart beating. With your eyes closed, you will start to feel things over your skin and imagine things that may be going on around you. You will try to reconstruct your environment because your brain wants to perceive your surroundings. It is said that dreaming is simply the brain's way of seeing when there are no physical constraints on its interpretations. Your brain does this without you consciously compelling it to do so.

When you are hearing a conversation, the same thing occurs. What you are receiving goes through a series of filters, all your dimensions, and searches for what it wants to hear and then pings an understanding to them through categorizing the information. Your brain stores the information in schemas and then can recall information based upon the connectivity of those schemas to other schemas. This is important for understanding because it is in those connections that you can devise empathy. You can train your brain to begin to understand the "point of view" that others may have. Allow yourself to imagine you as the person you are conferring with and imagine the options from that person's point of view. At that point, you can then understand someone else's ideology. In win-win, you should be listening all the time. Your brain will take over and do the rest.

In active sensing, you are applying an intention to your action. Hearing is passive, but when objectives are attached to it, it is then active listening. Hearing, speaking, feeling, seeing, and tasting, with intention to understand is how you can participate in the beginning of discussions. This becomes important when dealing with multiple parties. There will be plenty said, but there is also much said in silence. Use silence strategically. When you have an idea for what you are looking for in the group's verbal and non-verbal dialogue, it will become obvious to identify who in the group is uncomfortable and who is satisfied. Body language and unconscious reactions to words will all demonstrate the true progress towards a goal that is occurring by a group. There is also a sixth sense that you can develop after properly empathizing with another individual. You will be able to capture the vibes of how others are feeling about a particular topic. While you are actively participating, it is important to identify not only what another person is commenting on or demonstrating; you should also be aware of why that person may feel a certain way. This may be accomplished by prying deeper into how a person arrived at their created option, and what they feel could be gained or lost from choosing it.

By reading these vibes, you can do two things: one is a win-win approach on your individual basis, and the other is a win-win for the group. By mentioning that you understand their concerns, but you would like to let someone else offer their commentary on a particular topic, you will free the room to let the weaker personalities engage in discussion.

The second thing is to identify whether the options the group is offering are a win-win option. If not, then you can appropriately adjust the talking track so that everyone is focused on the same objective. Finally, when considering a win-win option and handling the discussion in a win-win manner, it is not necessary to give it the name "win-win". You should find some unique way to phrase how you feel about the solution and use that. (Branding, when done incorrectly, can be very dangerous and destructive to your reputation.) Discussion is not accomplished without understanding the other parties.

You can complete the chart to begin the process of understanding the other parties involved.

Party	Desired Outcome	Resource Required	Reason for Desire

III. **Shortcuts do not exist with a Win/Win mentality.**

There are no shortcuts to excellence. A shortcut is a perceivably shorter route to a destination than a more common one. Reasons people may take a common road over a shortcut include lack of knowledge, aversion to change, or risk involved in uncertainty. Metaphorically, it is an option that requires less time, effort, or resources than other options when accomplishing an objective. With a win-win mentality, understand there are no shortcuts. You will have to put effort into understanding others and develop the skill in shaping a win-win option. The result, however, will be one that not only promotes your agenda and well-being, but also creates inspired and loyal followers who will trust your reasoning and methods.

> Comprehension Exercise: Think of someone you have a difficult relationship with – what is it that they truly desire as an outcome and which of your abilities can assist in achieving that?

Resources

"The third character essential to Win/Win is the Abundance Mentality, the paradigm that there is plenty out there for everybody." **(7 HABITS OF HIGHLY EFFECTIVE PEOPLE)**

    A. <u>Compromising is not an option.</u>

There is always more to consider with a mentality of abundance. With a win-lose or lose-win mentality, the concern is that resources are finite or limited. The full spectrum of Abundance Mentality will come later but understand that when creating a win-win option, it is not simply a plan of compromise. It is a plan that considers as many facets as possible and attempts to achieve an objective while meeting the expectations of all parties. A compromise, on the other hand, qualifies as a shortcut. A compromise is a consequence of a win-lose mentality. "If I give some, then you can give some on your demands. We will sacrifice together for the greater good of a plan." Whereas a win-win says, "This plan benefits everyone, and for those who will be indirectly affected by it, it has created a way to still utilize their skills." Some may argue that the heightened use of technology has replaced jobs in our current economy and is partially to blame for the economic downturn. The win-win solution would consider these displaced workers, however, to further use and grow their skills in other ways. A compromise, on the other hand, may look like a severance package or unemployment benefits. The previously displaced workers would be out of luck in having a new job but could be paid for their previously completed work. The company would be able to lower their overhead costs by installing computers and laying off the workers. Here, both parties are temporarily content, but the workers are left pondering their utility and begin developing insecurities about their hiring value. Over time, these disgruntled workers may return to the company and protest the use of computers replacing jobs and stifling the economy. This becomes bad PR and bad PR can return low profit margins.

Here is another scenario. Perhaps, you are facing a situation where others have an interest in taking you out of power. A Win-lose option is to convince the others that they are wrong and that you are an asset to the group even though you know it is not true. A Lose-lose option is to destroy the entire team. A Lose-win option would be to acknowledge their request and step aside. A Win-win option involves a technique known as reconstructing the narrative. Reconstructing the narrative means to change the topic of discussion.

Usually, when all parties are represented within one group, each person focuses on their objectives or interests. As an effective leader, whether self-authorized or title-authorized, you must reconstruct the narrative. Identify a larger, more basic issue that is a common thread of agreement for all parties. Ask questions that help each person return to their vision/ interest building state and then begin to conjointly develop a new vision and a single objective. If this process, evident of a win-win, is not utilized, expect the discussion to devolve into either a stalemate or a compromise. Neither will get you what you desire. You can use questions such as:

    a.   How did we get to this point?
    b.   If we were to focus on one remedy, which department should that focus be channeled to and why?
    c.   What are some external consequences to our actions leading up to this meeting?
    d.   From where is our imbalance stemming?
    e.   Are there any other groups that are experiencing a similar problem?

Note: Make sure that everyone can answer. Be sure to present the image that everyone in the group is interdependent of each other. Everyone brings equal power to the discussion.

A resolution to the stated scenario may begin by questioning why your absence is imperative and identifying a way in which you can be an asset. Perhaps, letting you out of your current position, and occupying a different, more suitable position for your skill set will accomplish everyone's goals. Creating such an outlet allows the rest of the group to consider your talents elsewhere. Craft a vision around your option, and you will be sure to buy yourself some time and perhaps be happier.

    Resources Exercise: In what area do you believe you need additional resources? How can you apply abundance theory to that area and access resources from another source? Write it down.

Refinement

"Maturity is the balance between courage and consideration." **(7 HABITS OF HIGHLY EFFECTIVE PEOPLE)**

    B. It requires <u>maturity.</u>

Practice makes perfect. The practice of this mentality will refine you. You will know when to listen and when to speak. You will learn how to anticipate and identify the motivations of others. The application of this mentality, no matter how complex the circumstance is, requires maturity. Maturity is a psychological term that is used when describing one's ability to respond appropriately, or in a socially acceptable manner, in particular circumstances. One of the keys to maturity is control. Another is calculation. The last is empathy.

Control, in reference to maturity, is the ability to not act on an impulse and decide when and how to respond. Emotional control is perhaps the most difficult as emotions are innately present and fueled by our impulse to survive. If you feel threatened, rapid changes occur in your body to protect yourself. If you are in an environment that provides an imbalance of fear, love, or hope, you will be less able to adapt when the environment changes. Consistency breeds predictability which breeds comfort. Practice control by imagining and meditating on your responses in varying environments: encouraging, degrading, and unfulfilled promising. You will develop a stronger sense of yourself and your spectrum.

Calculation is more external. It requires measured decision making. Risk and reward-weighted decisions are involved in calculation. It is also prophetic in nature. Clearly, many of the parameters used for calculation can change in any given circumstance. This is especially true across diverse cultures. Some mannerisms are socially acceptable in the United States but are extremely taboo in the Middle East. Calculation requires time to learn about others and their expectations or norms.

Empathy is the intellectual identification with or vicarious experiencing of the feelings, thoughts, or attitudes of another. According to an etymology dictionary, "em-" means "in" and pathos means "feeling". Empathy is dependent on your ability to sense another's mindset and imagine the application of their circumstances to your life. Empathy goes beyond simply envisioning the words spoken, but to attach your own feelings associated with the presented circumstance. It can mean reliving the decisions and emotions the other individual made and felt. The result is not to excuse the other individual's behavior, but to empathize with it.

With these three facets (control, calculation, and empathy) in mind, you can develop your maturity and effectively apply the win-win mentality to any situation.

> Refinement Exercise: What are some areas where you can increase your maturity? Do you need to improve your control, calculation, or empathy?

Meditation Tenets

Creation defies the logic of scarcity as it can only be described by abundance. A creation or a thought of creation can be multiplied in it sharing. A theorem that shows that a possibility is to all possibilities.

Below are some questions that you should not quickly come to an answer for, but rather find some time to reflect upon. Consider the meaning of these questions (some have multiple meanings), and then meditate on your answers. When you have found your answer, it should feel honest and consistent with who you are.

1. Where might you practice win-win mentality?
2. In which areas have you subscribed to scarcity mentality? Why?
3. In which areas have you subscribed to abundance mentality? Why?
4. What would it take to move from a scarcity mentality to an abundance mentality?
5. Have you taken inventory of your assets?
6. Have you leveraged those assets to help you achieve a goal?
7. Have you taken the time to consider the thoughts and motivations of others?
8. Have you developed a plan for those things that present the greatest amount of stress in your life?

Week **Five**

It is prudent to have a goal for every action. Envisioning a future is a great source of motivation and will provide the appropriate reasons for cautiousness. This, in turn, will help with navigating around obstacles and opportunities. This week's chapter proposes the tools and friends needed to escort you to your desired future.

The Future

Note: "Substance means: that which underlies all outward manifestations; the essence; the essential reality; the thing in itself, etc. Substantial means: actually existing; being the essential element; being real, etc. Reality means: the state of being real; true, enduring; valid; fixed' permanent; actual, etc..." (Kybalion)

A substantial reality is a reality with considerable value or meaning, and when considering your future, it is the imperative way of imagining it. Something of substance indicates that it has meaning in realness. It is vivid or important. In law and in science, substantial evidence is persuasive, tangible, and maneuverable. Reality is existence. The substances that exist are the manifestations of ideas or the combination of elements to make an entity capable of interaction. To reference the dimensions, the Social Dimension is the manifestation of the Spiritual Dimension. The Substantial Reality is the Social Dimension that should be envisioned when reflecting on the Spiritual Dimension.

There are many uncertainties when considering the future, and we are always planning our lives based with it in mind, albeit the immediate, or the extended. One of the reasons that procrastination exists is because we acknowledge the existence of a future. We envision ourselves engaged in a task or in our dreams in the context of the future. Perhaps we dream of wealth, fame, or family. When we go about planning for what has yet to come to pass, we usually take tangible steps to have the envisioned substantial reality manifest. The same is true for every aspect of our lives. In planning for the future, however, there are a few ideas that should be considered.

The operational definitions for this chapter are below:

Vision is the act or power of sensing with the eyes or with sight and the act or power of anticipating that which will or may come to be.

A supervisor is one that directs or oversees a person, group, department, organization, or operation.

Super is a prefix occurring originally in loanwords from Latin, with the basic meaning "above, beyond." Words formed with super- have the following general senses: "to place or be placed above or over" (superimpose; supersede), "a thing placed over or added to another".

As trivial as it sounds, you should supervise your life. Super means "above or beyond", and vision is the act of seeing. So, the idea behind supervising your life is seeing beyond the current situation into the future. A supervisor looks over an entity of discussion. Imagine a map in which there is an outlined destination. From the top, you can see where the pathways are. You can compare the routes by length and time. You can see if there are obstacles in the routes, and plan to navigate the best possible route. Once the pathway has been understood, you can then travel the route and arrive at your designated destination. Now, imagine the route from one dimension, a front-end view. All you will be able to see are multiple paths and it will be nearly impossible to anticipate obstacles or compare possible routes.

As we navigate through life, we tend to focus on front-end views. What is going on right here and right now in my current situation? I am given a choice of going left or going right. I can jump over the fallen tree, or I can crawl under it. When we take an aerial view, however, the entire pathway becomes clearer and easier to maneuver. So, when being a supervisor, keep in mind that you are not simply looking at a situation, but you are looking beyond or above it. Using this approach in planning for the future will be positive for your leadership, both as a leader to yourself, and as a leader for others. Create a vision complete with a starting point and a destination. Then, follow it.

Things to consider about a vision....

I.   **You must have a goal.**

As in the case with the map, having a destination is vital to your success. Designating a destination allows you to evaluate your current position. Find a blank sheet of paper and draw two blocks: A and B. Make B your destination. Make A your initial point. Your B should be an end goal. Label your Point B with qualities. What does the B look like? Now, label your point A with its attributes. Your Point A answers, "What do you look like now?" and How would you describe your current state of being?" There is most likely a difference between the two, but this is one way to demonstrate that you can begin to plan how you can happen upon your destination. The end goal is the driving factor in the map and there are some special features to your point B.

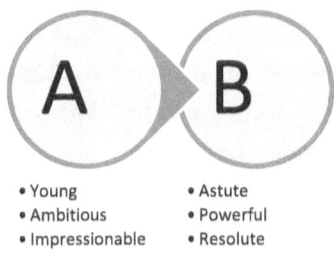

- Young
- Ambitious
- Impressionable

- Astute
- Powerful
- Resolute

The difference between the two points is translated into a path to get from Point A to Point B. The plan/map has many facets to its development which will be later discussed in the book.

Completion

"Do not go past the mark you aimed for; in victory, Learn when to stop. The moment of victory is often the moment of greatest peril. In the heat of victory, arrogance and overconfidence can push you past the goal you had aimed for, and by going too far, you make more enemies than you defeat. Do not allow success to go to your head. There is no substitute for strategy and careful planning. Set a goal, and when you reach it, stop." **(48 LAWS OF POWER)**

    A.   <u>I have a purpose.</u>

Your Point B is your purpose. The reason behind beginning the journey is to arrive at point B. It should be crafted with a permanent image in your mind. Having a point B in mind is extremely important as it will indicate where your planning stopped (plans are described in depth in Part Two of the Influence series). Going beyond Point B leaves much room for uncontrollable factors to play a part in your failure, as no precaution was taken. It is the same as landing a plane and then walking. Depending on where the plane landed, without additional information, your ability to survive and succeed is drastically compromised. As you near or once you arrive at your point B, it is a great time to pause and reflect on your direction and determine if additional planning is needed.

When crafting your Point B, you should use archetypes. If someone says, "Mother," an image comes to mind. This image is what can be known as an archetype. It is a universally acceptable and understood symbol and is usually associated with a standard. Some other archetypical words include:

Angel	President/ Leader
God	Brother
Politician	Mother
Queen/King	Father
Doctor	Prince/Princess
Judge	Artist
Jester	

While some of the associated standards that crop into the mind are not realistic, envisioning your end goal as an archetype will do much for establishing a vivid impression, or vision, of your Point B. The more completely Point B is described, the more realistic options you will have when it is time to configure the path.

Another consideration regarding your Point B is the interaction that it will have in the world. What is the perceived worth of a mosquito if it is not considered within its larger context which is in the world? It, of course, possesses inherent value, but it is not understood until after its interaction with other entities and lifeforms. Beyond simply creating an archetype, determine the value and worth by understanding the interactions that you will encounter at your destination. If you envision yourself as a chief executive officer of a large engineering firm, what kind of CEO are you? Are you actively involved in product development, do you handle negotiations around the world, and where do your contracts come from? Are you patient, impatient, liked or feared? What does your large firm produce or manufacture? What conversations might you have daily? What would you be expected to understand or know? What is your expertise? Is your company providing a large benefit to others and what is their annual profit margin? What would you do with the profits? Would they be retained earnings or help fund charities? How do you make decisions? Build the image of your destination so well that it almost seems tangible. Do this so that it may begin to manifest into a substantial reality. It is akin to planting seeds in the Spiritual Dimension, watering in the Mental Dimension, pruning in the physical Dimension, and harvesting in the Social Dimension.

Your Point B should be a culmination of all your four dimensions. If your spiritual, mental, physical, or social parameters contradict each other, you will be destined for failure. You should use these dimensions to further explore your chosen archetype(s) and dwell on your actual beliefs. Many people can articulate their visions, but very few can truly *identify* with their visions on all levels. Are you designed properly to become your chosen archetype? Which weaknesses will cause you to be ineffective? Can you physically handle or input the work required to make your vision become a substantial reality? Do you believe that the archetype plays a vital and necessary role? Is the role in accordance with the beliefs you have about how the world works?

To the extent that you can align your four dimensions can be understood as the true concept of individuality. You were created specifically and uniquely by intention or by chance. What you offer is different from others because many factors are involved in determining your current state. How, where, and when you were raised are all important in determining your purpose.

So, if you find yourself jealous of another, then take a moment to reflect on your own possessions. It is not that they are more valuable than you. The truth is that you provide a value in a different form. Although food is important, man cannot live on bread alone. He must have many other things that provide value for his life to be fulfilled. He needs water and love. If love were jealous of water and water jealous of love (the thought is humorous), then what world would we be in? As a side note, jealousy will prevent your individual growth and create discord in your life. Quickly identify your jealousies and begin to explore your own individuality so that you may more completely envision your purpose and appreciate your uniqueness.

Completion Exercise: Make of list of the projects of yours are incomplete, and why? Then write down what completion means and what resource is needed to complete it.

Ethic

"'How did you learn to read?' the girl asked at one point. "Like everybody learns,' he said, 'In school.' 'Well, if you know how to read why are you just a shepherd?'" **(The Alchemist)**

B.   I have roles to fulfill.

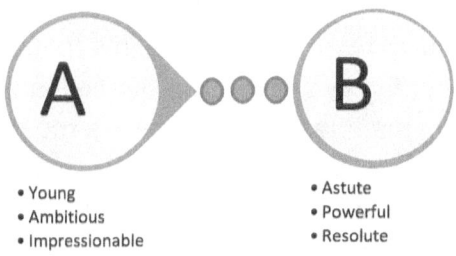

- Young
- Ambitious
- Impressionable

- Astute
- Powerful
- Resolute

Recognize that the process between points A and B involves occupying many roles. Roles are temporary positions that you fill within the context of achieving your purpose. If willed, there is a reason to every role that you occupy. This quote references an incident in The Alchemist in which a seemingly poor shepherd boy is reading. The girl interrogates him due to the cognitive dissonance of seeing a shepherd boy reading as reading was a skill associated with wealth or a higher status. The lesson to understand in this part of the book is the importance of occupying a role and the humility associated with the occupancy of that role. Perhaps you intend to be the world's most important leader. You are, however, currently a janitor. This does not mean that you are traveling the wrong path, or that the current job is beneath you. You should view it as a stage, however. It is a level in which you must obtain necessary attributes and relationships for you to arrive at your destination. Regarding the travel metaphor to a destination, each role is as a gas stop is to arriving at the final destination. You must fuel yourself, and you cannot be partially fueled. Along the way, you will have to stop and ask for directions, fuel your car, and learn your environment so that you can navigate along the streets. The aerial view will allow you to navigate yourself correctly, but you still must drive the route you plan.

So, in the case of the reading shepherd, the books he read and the skill to read became pivotal for his eventual arrival at his "personal legend". He ended the story with a family and wealth, but he learned much on his journey through filling the roles of a shepherd, a tribal constituent, a merchant's assistant, and many others. Each role then proceeded to assist with the next. The same is true for your life. There are roles you play, such as: child, parent, student, worker, manager, etc. You should be willing to embrace your current role and maximize the opportunities within that role by learning the craft that is being taught. If you are teaching someone, learn how to teach to the best of your ability. Envision yourself excelling in every role you partake in. You should understand the terms of your role. What is expected of you, what do you have the capability of doing, and what are you willing to do? You should take the time to develop your work ethic and ability to build relationships. You should be an asset to whomever you enter a relationship with so as to develop their dependency on you and to gain the most out of that relationship.

The other element to this quote is condescending encouragement. The girl ends by saying, "Well then why are you just a shepherd?" While her question could be interpreted to mean 'you could do so much more since you can read', the tone of the phrase means: you are wasting your time reading if all you are going to be is a shepherd. The latter is usually construed as discouragement, especially if we have no control over whether we are a shepherd or not. Retrain yourself, however, to understand the value that is inherent within every role. The boy understood his value by replying with the importance of learning how to care for things that were dependent upon his guidance. Sheep cannot tell the difference between safe grounds to feed and those with danger. A shepherd, however, works long days and ensures the safety of his sheep by staying aware of the surroundings and protecting them from potential predators. His reward is based on the health and survival of his flock. Do not take your life experiences for granted as they will be needed on recall for the rest of your life. If you had a poor childhood, realize that you experienced it for a reason. The qualities you can develop during such a phase will be important for your success in the future.

II.   **You must see the journey.**

When planning your future, it is imperative that you not only envision your Point A and your Point B but envision the journey in between. Imagine the types of obstacles you will encounter, and what you will have to learn along the way. Envision which pathways will lead you to your Point B from your Point A. As Alice in Wonderland was wandering through her forest, she encountered all sorts of puzzles, traps, and interesting characters. Your life will not be too different. If you plan to attain massive amounts of wealth, the journey will be filled with multiple roadblocks and traps. Financial gimmicks and dream gurus will try to test your patience and sense of hope or faith that will lead you down a path of misery. Individuals who specialize in mind games will play them on you: stalling techniques, tools of propaganda and persuasion, and too-good-to-be true deals claiming to be free of charge. People will present shortcuts that are filters in disguise. They filter out individuals who:

1) Do not know their worth.
2) Have no intent on developing a true ethic.
3) Are not sure of what they want, need, or love.
4) Are seeking shortcuts because of the fear associated with failing.

You should not blame the crafty individuals you meet. They are blessings in disguise reminding you of where you could or should be. They are doing what they do best. Blame yourself for falling prey to one of the four types. Fix it and move on.

> Ethic Exercise: What shortcuts do you currently engage in? Make a list and determine which of the four filters are causing you to adopt the shortcut.

Approach

"Plan all the way to the end: The ending is everything. Plan all the way to it, taking into account all the possible consequences, obstacles, and twists of fortune that might reverse your hard work and give glory to others. By planning to the end you will not be overwhelmed by circumstances and you will know when to stop. Gently guide fortune and help determine the future by thinking far ahead." **(48 Laws of Power)**

    A.   <u>I must understand the playing field.</u>

To safeguard yourself from those four individual types, you must understand the rules of the game which you are playing a hand. Imagine your friends want to play Monopoly. When you all sit down, you try to apply the rules of chess. The result is inefficiency. I doubt the game could even be started, and perhaps an evening of teasing and arguing would follow such idiocy. This idea is also captured in the quote: "If you only have a hammer, everything looks like a nail." Seems simple enough, but when we return to our lives, we sometimes forget that just because we may recognize that a game is being played, all scenarios do not play the same game. The rules change, and it would work to your advantage to be flexible and privy to the rules that govern the games. If you know what a politician is doing (you learn this from the use of empathy from the previous chapter), then you can interpret "between the line" speeches.

Playing fields are systems in their entirety: the involved parties, processes, and expected reaction-action orders. It would be a fallacy to assume that all systems operate under the same ethics. So, when viewing the pathways from Point A to Point B, you can understand each pathway's intricacy by observing its associated rules. In Alice in Wonderland, this is also evident- although ironic.

Clearly, however, there are some basic assumptions that can be made for all playing fields. Almost all our systems are directly related to the three main emotions of humans: love, hope, and fear. They are all related to a need for survival. From there, the conclusions to the assumptions begin to change. There are some who think of self-preservation. Others have divided themselves in a way to think of the survival of larger groups of people. When a person feels threatened, there are a range of reactions that they can follow. Know who you are dealing with so that you can best anticipate their moves. If they have been trained, be cautious. In business, there is a difference between meeting someone who is seasoned, and a first-year student. On average, it would be much easier to play mind games on one of them. Much of the planning process will come from applying the chapters Win-Win Mentality (Week 4) and The Plan (Week 9).

When this quote references "all the way to the end", it is referencing your Point B. Envisioning how a pursuit may twist and turn is very important, and recognizing the interacting orders is vital to your success. *"Gently guiding fortune"* is a technique. You should never be too outlandish in your pursuits. It will breed insecurities in bystanders. Just as you get jealous, others do too. When you excel, you remind others of their inadequacies. Gently guiding involves a careful and calculated method of achieving goals. There should be a rhyme and reason to your success that others can easily grasp and partake in. Beyond just following paths, you can change them. You can add and take away where necessary, but it must be a calculated action. Organic happenings are subject to Darwin's survival of the fittest. You are giving "chance", which is unrecognized order, power to influence a situation. A win-win mentality will allow you the maximum protection from the interference of "chance" because of its planning-heavy techniques.

> Approach Exercise: Do you agree with having a win-win mentality? Why or why not? When and when not? Do you believe in Abundance Theory? Why or why not? When and when not? Write down the areas where you do not.

Certainty

"Enter action with boldness: If you are unsure of a course of action do not attempt it. Your doubts and hesitations will infect your execution. Timidity is dangerous: Better to enter with boldness. Any mistakes you commit through audacity are easily corrected with more audacity. Everyone admires the bold; no one honors the timid." **(48 LAWS OF POWER)**

B. <u>I will be making life-changing decisions.</u>

As a leader, you will be making many decisions. Every decision has a cause and an effect associated with it. This causal relationship will influence entities that you may not even be aware of. When justifying your path and making changes to it, realize that these changes have effects associated with them. Most of them will strongly impact your life. They may work to increase your options, or to limit your opportunities, but you should keep a mental ledger that accounts for your decisions.

When making decisions, you should be cautious, but when communicating your decisions, you should be bold. If you indicate any doubt in your communication, your followers will begin to doubt you. Your confidence will strengthen those who listen, and even if you are wrong in your statement, another strong statement will mitigate the effects of a bad decision. To accomplish such boldness, you should spend time reflecting on your decision before you communicate it. You should convince yourself that the option you are deciding to follow is the option you agree with 100%. When it is time for you to deliver your decision, everyone will have open ears because it will be obvious that you are committed to your decision, and for many, that is a prerequisite for its success. The reason this is subliminally true, is because boldness is tied into the ego. To save face, the audience perceives that you will try to do everything in your power to prove that your decision was the correct decision. If someone asks you, "Do you want to do this job?", and you have decided you do, your answer is, "I would be happy to do this job, because I know the value that I will bring to you and your project or team." Be bold.

Unfortunately, the way to beat a lie detector is to really believe your lies. Such control requires much reflection because with words alone, you cannot get away with lying. Your body will betray you. Your heart rate increases, your brain starts using its creative side, and you become sweaty. Your voice quivers, your eyes rummage, and your veins thicken because of the increased pressure. Your words begin to stumble on top of each other because you begin speaking too quickly. You realize it and so you try to slow your speech down, making your listener feel uncomfortable and question your intentions. Your listener identifies what is occurring and walks away remarking how they feel uncomfortable around you and thus, they do not trust you. Communicating a decision is an art. If you do not believe in your decision enough, your body will communicate it as though it were a lie. Others will believe it to be so, too. It should be said with enough concreteness and conciseness that there is no room to pull it apart before being considered. It should also be said encouragingly and objectively enough so as not to offend the listener. The balance is confidence, and not arrogance or reticence. Arrogance and reticence are consequences of an insecure individual who evaluates their worth comparatively with the worth of others. Confidence, however, is conveyed without words.

III. You must have friends for your journey.

Of course, when thinking about your future, there are several things you will need. One of which is friends. They are reliable to a certain point and will be essential on your pursuits. There are two kinds of friends that you should have on your journey. Any others are not necessarily friends, but acquaintances. The more friends you have, the more complex your planning will become. Strategic usage of your friends will allow you to manage an extremely successful journey. Once an individual becomes a friend, there is nothing which prevents them from converting back to being an acquaintance. At that point, their actions will solely consider their interests, and not those of the relationship. You should not blame a friend for tending to their personal desires, but you should be aware of a particular friend's predisposition or susceptibility to reverting outside of the friend relationship.

The friendship should work to the benefit of both who decide to enlist in the agreement, as mentioned with the win-win mentality. Interests and objectives should be clear, and susceptibilities can usually be configured from these initial interactions. Constantly evaluate your friends for their allegiance and reaffirm their comfort with your allegiance. There will be circumstances in which you will be on the lookout for your own interest, and not the interests of your friends. You should know what circumstance may get you to that point and know your friend's points.

To create a friend, communicate an image of the relationship in the beginning. Speak in vague words and experiences to find alignment with hopes, fears, and loves. This will open the door for them to also share their hopes, fears, and loves with you. Never tell all the details all at once. Details will usually betray the symbiotic relationship as conflicts will emerge, and you will ruin any prior progress made. As a friend demonstrates their interest, slowly share some details to encourage them to be even better friends. In this manner, you will always keep a repertoire of friends, but will protect yourself from acquaintances. It is not good for a leader to be alone. A lone leader goes unchecked and usually functions under clouded judgment because he is constantly trying to understand why he is alone. It is distracting. As a matter of fact, when you meet a lone leader, you can befriend him by speaking in terms of fear and hope.

> Certainty Exercise: Think about a decision where you are unsure of yourself. Reflect on your decision and commit by ensuring you have thought of as many variables as possible, and that you have done your best. Demonstrate to yourself that you are committed to your decision by acting in it today in some way. Remove the desire to succumb to a shortcut.

Apprenticeship

"Quite obvious to you at this point a mentor is someone who guides or trains a pupil at some skill or craft." **(YOUNG LEADER)**

    A.   <u>I have a mentor.</u>

One kind of friend you must have is a mentor. The only way you may have a map to use in aerial view is because of the mentors with whom you surround yourself. The concept is the same with charting topography. It requires another item or person to view and map the ground. A satellite may run a signal and use the change in speed of the return signal to map out what is in the nearby area. Books are the metaphorical equivalent of satellites as they are entities that can give you an abundance of information about a particular subject. Keep in mind that books are written by people. Authors have lives and opinions, and many times these experiences can bleed through the text. Knowing the author and their background is just as important as knowing the content of the book. It can help you with discriminating between advice worth using and advice worth reading. Some opinions may not apply, but there is deeper insight you can gain by knowing that the opinion exists. Some books provide greater insight into the meaning that other books are trying to convey. Missing out on a good book will limit your fluidity in traversing your pathway.

Many times, in the metaphor of the satellite, people are sent to ensure that the satellite is gathering accurate information. They verify the accuracy by walking the actual land mass and mapping steep or gradient inclines and discriminating between water and land areas. They then either confirm the findings or establish new information for the map. Before a golf course can be used, engineers approach the green and use lasers to properly classify each hole by par and ensure that the actual green matches the expected green. The point here is that maps are only made after being reviewed first. A mentor is someone who has traversed some part of your figurative map and can provide you with details on its figurative layout and features. Mentors are the first type of friend when travelling on your journey to your future. A complete version of a map is only possible after consulting many different topographers. This is also true of your life journey. A clear vision of it is only possible once you have been given consultation from mentors.

The map is made after walking it a few times. Use your mentors to make the task more efficient. When learning from others, there are a few particulars to keep in mind. Firstly, the information being given may have inherent faults. Perhaps a company's topographer was only able to walk four feet into a new territory before he was quickly captured by natives in the area. Since he was taken hostage, the company sent another topographer. He traveled another route to avoid the natives but ran out of things to eat and so the company had to rescue him. Then, a third topographer entered the territory through another clearing. All three will have similar information to give you about the territory and there will also be differences. The one taken as a hostage will probably tell you to never enter the territory. The second will probably say you must bring a lot of food with you so as not to starve. The third will give you the topography surrounding only one pathway and tell you that it is probably the best path since he made it through without any problems. While all pieces of information may be true, they also are equally likely to be only true in certain instances. It is up to you to be able to practice discernment with the advice of mentors. They are speaking to you in terms of their lives and experiences, which may only be similar to yours. A true map of the territory would come from listening to the similarities in their stories. In scientific testing, when using multiple data points, Analyses of Variance (ANOVAs) are performed to cross-analyze results. An ANOVA will determine whether a specific result occurred enough to be viewed as a cause and not a random correlation. An example is demonstrated below:

Experiment One
A coin is flipped once, and a thunderstorm occurs.
The conclusion is that whenever a coin is flipped, a thunderstorm occurs.

Experiment Two
A coin is flipped 10,000 times, and each time, a thunderstorm occurs, yielding 10,000 thunderstorms in the same place.

For the first Experiment, the ANOVA would show that there is a high chance that the two occurrences only happened by chance, and not necessarily a result of a direct cause-effect relationship. For the second experiment, however, the ANOVA would indicate a very small variance between the results and show that there is a high chance that the first occurrence is the direct cause of the other. When cross analyzing the wisdom of others, it is important to do mental ANOVAs. What are the chances of detail "A" being accurate and under which circumstances does that direct relationship occur? If you do not sort out the incongruences of your mentors, and blindly apply all their advice regardless of validity, then you will have to accept the consequences of those imprudent actions. You cannot blame others for your failings in discernment. Tread carefully, as it is your life, and you only live this life once. Regardless, mentors are an invaluable asset when taking your journey. There are no bad mentors, only an array of mentors. You can learn something from anyone. Sorting through the advice they give may be difficult, but you must be willing to spend time analyzing the risks involved in your decisions. Then, be bold with your decisions.

If you do not take the time to sort through the information that a mentor may give you, then you will eventually make decisions you do not wholeheartedly believe in. Once this happens, you will hold grudges against your mentors for "forcing" you to make certain decisions. It is best to determine who you are and what you want before immediately taking the advice of a mentor. If you do happen to make a decision that concludes poorly, then you must accept ultimate responsibility for it. If you blame another person for your actions, you will never grow or learn, and will only reaffirm that you have limitations within your ability to make decisions. You will erode your confidence in future circumstances.

> Apprenticeship Exercise: Who are your mentors and advocates? Is there anyone you can seek out that lives a life similar to what you would like to live? Does that lifestyle create a sense of purpose? Is consistent with your standards? Is it based in pursuing your ideal self? If not, create an opportunity to meet someone like that by being where they might be. This relationship should come with work that forces you to move towards your point B.

Practice

"Empowerment can best be explained as the distribution of power onto others in a way that allows them to create an even stronger power base for themselves." **(Young Leader)**

   B. I have a mentee.

As you learn something new, it is important to practice it. "Practice makes perfect". The adage is prevalent because it is true. To practice the new information you gain from mentors, you can do two things: meditate and find a friend to mentor.

When meditating, you are searching through your life and identifying where you can make personal improvements and position your strengths and passions. You are effectively treating yourself as a mentee. In this process, you should be reflecting on your past and current circumstances and trying to apply new wisdom to old situations. Empathize with your past so that you can become aware of your own judgments and justifications. It is here where you can learn to anticipate yourself and control your tendencies.

With mentoring, you can express your newly devised wisdom to another, and discover its manifestation into a substantial reality. If your advice works, then your mentees should thrive. They should benefit from your wisdom. If they falter, however, then chances are you should review your current mindset and aptitude to apply wisdom.

Feedback received from your mentee can take one of two forms: positive or negative. In mentorship, you should share your ideologies. Your mentees will learn from your habits and the things you do not say, however. It is akin to creating a mirror. You can gain greater understanding of yourself and correct your mentee by correcting yourself. You can also commend yourself by commending your mentee. With mentees, be sure to practice patience and empathy. These friends are the most loyal because they are dependent upon your wisdom. They assume you have their best interest in mind, and you should do your utmost not to abuse it. Mentees are very valuable and can become your future bodyguards when you are successful.

A caveat with the mentee relationship is that you can spurn them and create enemies. This technique can be used both to your advantage and your disadvantage, but either option is a possibility. If a mentee feels betrayed, they will hold a grudge against you and work against you. Be sure to disseminate open-ended and multilateral advice so as not to have a mentee feel pressured to accept it. If you become too engrossed in their affairs and convince them to accept advice which then turns awry, the first person they will blame is you, their mentor, for "making them do it".

IV.   You must have tools.

Beyond books, there are many other tools that you can use when preparing for your future and venturing on your journey. Recall, this entire theme is regarding how to view the world. It explores which kinds of logic and emotions should be applied to circumstances, your approach, and what the future represents. The future is the manifestation of your four dimensions and is your substantial reality. The more vividly you imagine your future to be, the more of a substantial reality it can potentially become. Your future will become your way of life as you will develop a second nature muscle in identifying trends and opportunities that will keep your present full of adventure and new learning experiences. You have already established a few mental tools within this theme, and a tool that can be consulted as a mentor. As a refresher, the mental tools are:

1)   An aerial view of your journey

This skill is difficult and requires the active use of information provided by mentors. Practicing involves thinking in the long term. If you are making a decision, ask, "How does it affect you one year from now?"

What are some potential hazards and risks involved by deciding one way or another? Who will benefit and who will be harmed? Does this decision get me closer to my end game, my Point B, my purpose?

2) The ability to judge yourself from the outside (to step outside of your body since you have a dual nature).

With children, this concept is known as Theory of Mind. Most people do not develop it until the age of four, but it is having the ability to understand that other viewpoints exist. The same reason a child believes that his mother is the only mother that exists is because he assumes his life and standards are the only ones that exist.

An experiment was performed with a group of students in determining their ability to logically approach a problem or question from the viewpoint of another. A teddy bear was seated next to the first child. A box of crayons was displayed for the child. The box was opened, revealing crayons. When the box was closed, the child was asked what was in the box. The child remarked, "Crayons." The child was then asked, what does the teddy bear think is in the box?" The child remarked, "Crayons."

The teddy bear was then removed from the area. Next, the crayons in the box were replaced with a new item. The child was asked what was inside of the box. The child responded with the name of the new item. Then, the teddy bear was brought back into the room. The child was asked what the teddy bear thought was inside of the box. The child responded again with the name of the new item. The results of the experiment overwhelmingly went this way until the researchers tested children over the age of four. These children overwhelmingly responded that the teddy bear would think the crayons were in the box and not the new item because the teddy bear did not "see" when the items were exchanged.

Our ability to think like another, or experience as another does, is a developed skill, and can continue to be developed.

While these tools are great for establishing a journey, there are still some tools to use on your journey that must be discussed.

> Practice Exercise: Before confronting a situation or event where you must demonstrate excellence, imagine yourself walking or going through it. Pick an upcoming milestone or event coming up in your life. Practice in your mind what you might encounter with your five senses. What do you hear, how do you feel, what are the scents, what do you see, and what is your emotional state? Experience the event before the event and prepare yourself for what may come by anticipating all that may occur.

Forces

"Conserve our forces and energies by keeping them concentrated at their strongest point. You gain more by finding a rich mine and mining it deeper, than by flitting from one shallow mine to another- intensity defeats extensity every time. When looking for sources of power to elevate you, find the one key patron, the fat cow who will give you milk for a long time to come."
(48 Laws of Power)

A.   I know my resources.

Many people use a lack of resources as an excuse for not accomplishing their goals. These resources could include relationships, money, objects, people of desire, land, necessities, education, social status, appearance, genetic makeup, intimate elements, mediums of communication, loyal followers, or a support infrastructure (network). Resources are influenced by forces, which are motivations behind the four dimensions (More in Week 7). How well we allocate resources is a testament to how we view the value of our resources and our possession of them. By focusing the forces to a single point of interest, you can create a goal that is aligned on all levels and increase the chances of succeeding in that goal. When you focus on something, your mind is obsessively concerned about it. As with a man who has a hammer, all things look like nails, opportunities will be easy to spot because you are focused on a goal with a method in mind. Your win-win mentality and four-dimensional perspective should not be compromised by your focus, but they should rather guide your focus. As a lens guides the light to the inner workings of your eyes, so will your forces guide your focus, so that it may be seen more clearly.

Resources should be strategically positioned. You must keep in mind that others who need resources will seek to have yours. The goal is not to be stingy with your possessions, but to be critical about who receives them. Understand what they will do with your resources and be careful when completely absolving yourself of the sovereignty of your belongings. While you may have used your resources wisely, the receiver may have no intention of doing the same.

The other element to this section is in the search for resources. If possible, it is better to find one source that provides much than many sources that provide little. The exception to this is when you are seeking the vested interest of many. In this scenario, you want all participants to have some risk involved with a transaction so that the total risk is distributed. Any deal without risk to a buyer is likely to be abused. Finding one source, a true patron, can be very useful. Patrons usually give you more than one resource. They can provide monetary gain, status, and a network. In exchange, you must perform services at the whim of the patron. If you have two or more patrons, interests become more complicated. This is not to say that you should not have multiple streams of income, but stay focused on your end goal, and utilize your resources so that you may accomplish it.

Resources can be used in multiple ways:

End-Goal Obtainment

Resources can be directly used to buy a house, or stage an event, or win an election. Most people think of money this way, "When I get rich or wealthy, I am going to…" While the notion is filled with hope and keeps the short- and long-term goals conscious, it is not the complete vision of resource utilization. This is the most prevalent mechanism by which we view resources, and it causes us to excuse ourselves from accomplishing our goal through steps that could be taken today. It also provides us with comfort in knowing the civic and personal good we may one day do with a lot of money. At the end of the day, however, what is done with a little is what a person does with a lot. If you can be a great steward of a mediocre salary, then you have a greater chance of being a great steward of a large salary. Set resource goals and apply your resources to accomplishing small things if you only have a small amount. If you have a large amount, do the same. Never catch yourself disseminating resources you do not yet have. It is a sure way for others to take advantage of you. If you are in debt, it means your value has been negatively valued. That is enough of a weakness for another individual to offer you a deal you cannot refuse, and then you must owe them. There are many discussions involving good debt and bad debt, but in general, having outstanding resource promises holds you subject to someone or some entity. Even your citizenship does not come freely. So, as you are handling your resources, identify what resources can be applied to short-term goals, and then accomplish those short-term goals. Practicing this with just a little will leave the door open for having more later. Not to mention, in the process, you are accomplishing goals.

System Influence

Resources are also used to influence a system. Salaries are paid to incentivize workers to do a specific job. Bribes are used for either protection or a guaranteed contract. Resources are used to do this because the global nature of resources is that they are always in demand. Someone else wants your land and sees a specific value in it. Therefore, you may be the happy medium for them to accomplish their end goal. The transaction of resources represents the transactions of interest. Much can be learned about an individual once they have been asked what they are looking to exchange. Imagine hostage situations. The first question in negotiation is, "What are your demands?" These demands are then analyzed to understand motives and willingness to carry out a threat. Resources can be used to influence a system, and this is what is known as leverage or power. When you have something to offer that is in demand and of limited accessibility, you have leverage, and the effective power to have your interests met. This is one of the reasons why you should understand your unique talents and offerings so that you may find yourself more influential. "Power" can be understood to mean having insight into a system. If you can understand a system, you can directly influence the system. Your actions with leveraging will have a ripple effect that you should not only be aware of, but deliberately use.

Resource Pool Growth

The final usage of resources includes growing a smaller set of resources to a larger amount. This transaction is usually known as investing. In investing, resources of a certain value are strategically applied to attract more resources or increase in value. Investment styles are very personal and, at a minimum, require some analysis of risk, and additionally the use of intuition. Numbers, if tortured enough, can be made to say anything. So having an intuitive sense for how a system works would be much to your benefit. True intentions can be hidden behind a great display of puppetry. To understand your resource pool or its ability to grow, seek out mentors and convince them to help you as a mentee, by soon becoming a prodigy of theirs. There is much to learn about gatekeepers in Week 19.

> Forces Exercise: Think back to the Completion Exercise. How would you like to use your resources once you obtain them? What is your primary goal with those resources? Is it to store them? Do

you seek to share them? How would you like to share them? Will you use them to create a specific outcome? Which gatekeepers possess these resources that you need?

Gifts

"So here are a few things that can be considered traits of creativity: 1. Ability to relate a vision. 2. Talent in some unique way. 3. Recognition that there's art in just about everything. 4. Desire to be fantastic." **(Young Leader)**

    B.   <u>I know my creations.</u>

The final tools you have on your journey are your own creations. These are the entities or circumstances that you manufacture with your resources. You should know what you can create and use those skills in your job. Note that any learned skill can in some way, shape, or form be applied to any job. What qualifies as a creation? Manufactured works that require creativity are included in the definition of a creation. The quote proposes a few guidelines for determining creativity. The first is the ability to relate a vision. Realize that everything you envision is created in your mind. You understand it well because you thought of it. However, when communicating the vision to another person, you are required to understand how the person would be able to understand it too. Imagine if you and another individual spoke two different languages. You could not simply explain your thoughts to the other person using your language. You must be creative in relating your vision. Perhaps a translator is needed, or you can use pictures. Maybe, you learn their language and the language's nuances to clearly describe your vision. Whatever the transaction requires, in translating a vision from yourself to another, you must be creative.

Another way to look at creativity is through a particular talent. A talent is some act that you perform that is either superlative to or different from others. Talents can be used for bad or for good, but they are a part of your creativity. The most common forms of talent that are associated with creativity are those within the arts: writing, drawing, painting, singing, speaking, etc. You can also have a talent in advising people in their affairs as a good consultant or counselor. Talents are diverse and span a vast array in kinds. How you use them is where creativity is important. Attaching value to a talent requires creativity. Painting is only important because we ascribe it to the value that has been presented in it. If a talent is no longer creating wealth, it is imperative to be creative and reconstruct the values associated with the talent. At one point, we had a need for draftsmen. Then, once computer programs were created to do the same job in at least half the time with twice the quality, the value associated with the profession of being a draftsman was severely diminished. The idea is not to give up and curse the system for devaluing your talent, but to get creative with your talent and make it invaluable. That is creativity.

Art exists in everything. There is an ebb and flow to all systems, manufactured and organic. Understanding the ebbs and flows will offer you the opportunity to be creative. The ebb and flow are present in the design and the building blocks of all systems. If you are looking at the human race's emotional system, an individual's ebb and flow is a building block of the larger system. You can run a campaign utilizing the human mob mentality by understanding how an individual can feel pressured into thinking a certain way. Using your knowledge of systems is a form of creativity.

Finally, a desire to be fantastic is pivotal. If you have the desire to be fantastic, that means you are constantly seeking opportunities to turn your resources into creations on your journey, and to do it efficiently and intently. Being in this mindset is a definite trait of a creative person. Fantastic people are always trying to expand their horizons and heighten their ceilings through the creative allocation and focusing of resources.

Creativity and resource management are essential for your journey. Maintain a clear perspective of your journey by taking an aerial view and seeking mentors to help define the pathways of the journey. Do not be afraid to be bold with your decisions, especially if you have spent sufficient time imagining your Point B and envisioning what you want. Your future depends on the decisions you make today and the mindset you carry with you along the way.

> Gifts Exercise: What have you created that you can use for your journey to your Point B? How do they relate? Write them down.

Meditation Tenets

The future is like a rain cloud on the horizon filled with unpredictability and consistency. It shall loom, cover, linger, and pass. It brings great news and death. The birds sing out to the clouds before and after; be in the best position to receive its blessings.

Below are some questions that you should not quickly come to an answer for, but rather find some time to reflect upon. Consider the meaning of these questions (some have multiple meanings), and then meditate on your answers. When you have found your answer, it should feel honest and consistent with who you are.

1. What does your point B look like? What characteristics do you possess?
2. What tools do you possess that can assist in your journey?
3. Who are your friends?
4. What have you created to further your journey?
5. When and how can you incorporate opportunities to move toward your point B?

Congratulations!

To My Wonderfully Committed Reader:

You have completed Part I! I hope to meet you at Part II to embark on the journey to dive deep into learning "How Do I Play a Role". I hope over the last 5 weeks you have already found new ways to be encouraged and are clearer on which direction you would like to go. I also hope that you have found new ways to tackle complex problems you may encounter in your relationships. Please visit the website to learn more about Influence and dive in deeper on Part I content. You can also find upcoming events in your area. The following pages provide a list of books that were used for the entire 25 Week series.

With much love and hope!

Credit is extended to...

7 Habits of Highly Effective People, Stephen Covey

10 Day MBA, Steven Siblinger

33 Strategies of War, Robert Greene

36 Stratagems, Book of Qi, Various Authors

48 Laws of Power, Robert Greene

Abundance, Peter Diamandis and Steven Kotler

The Alchemist, Paulo Coelho

The Arcane Teaching, William Walker Atkinson

Archetypes and the Collective Unconscious, Carl Jung

Arthashastra, Kautilya

Art of Seduction, Robert Greene

Art of War, Sun Tzu

As a Man Thinketh, James Allen

Audacity of Hope, President Barack Obama

Be the Leader You Were Meant to Be, Leroy Eims

The Bible, King James Version, Various Authors

The Black Hole War, Leonard Susskind

Brain Rules, John Medina

CEO Logic, C. Ray Johnson

Decision Points, President George W. Bush

The Elements of Moral Philosophy, James Rachels and Stuart Rachels

The Five Temptations of a CEO, Patrick Lencioni

Game Change, John Heilemann and Mark Halperin

Go Tell it on the Mountain, James Baldwin

How to Win Friends and Influence People, Dale Carnegie

Incidents in the Life of a Slave Girl, Harriet Jacobs

Kabbalah, Various Authors

A Kick in the Seat of the Pants, Roger VonOech

The Kybalion, The Three Initiates, Various Authors

The Masterkey System, Charles F. Haanel

Mind Manipulation, Dr. Haha Lung and Christopher Prowant

Mis-Education of the Negro, Carter G. Woodson

The Neurology of Thinking, D. Frank Benson

Power of the Subconscious Mind, Joseph Murphy

The Prince, Niccolo Machiavelli

The Quran, Various Authors

Rhetoric, Aristotle

The Secret, Rhonda Byrne

A Spiritual Treasury, Kahlil Gibran

Solution Selling, Keith M. Eades

Smart Women Finish Rich, David Bach

To Be Young, Gifted, and Black, Lorraine Hansberry and James Baldwin

Warfighting, U. S. Marine Corps Staff

The Wave, Todd Strasser

The World is Flat, Thomas Friedman

Young Leader, Nick Tarant

These books may or may not have been directly quoted or used, but their considerations were involved in the composition of this book. Some of the content expressed in this book directly contradicts what is within some of the credited books. The materials above were read, some in their entirety and others in piecewise fashion, and then analyzed to devise a way to communicate primary lessons alongside commentary provided by the author. Please note:

> *The philosophy in the book is predicated on the teachings of a broad panoply of literature. Influences from religions, concepts from various philosophers, biographies of the wealthy, and the lessons of the criminalized are all put into perspective in this 25 Week Journey.*

Bibliography

Carnegie, D. (2009). How to Win Friends and Influence People, Dale Carnegie, Arthur R. Pell, Dorothy Carnegie.

Coelho, P. (2006). The Alchemist, HarperCollins.

Covey, S. (1989). 7 Habits of Highly Effective People.

Covey, S. (1989). 7 Habits of Highly Effective People: Powerful Lessons in Personal Change, Free Press.

Eims, L. (2002). Be the Leader You Were Meant to Be, Chariot Victor Pub.

Gibran, K. (2008). A Spiritual Treasury, Oneworld.

Greene, R. (2000). 48 Laws of Power, Penguin Books.

Greene, R. (2004). "Art of Seduction." 468.

Initiates, T. T. (2008). The Kybalion, Jeremy P. Tarcher/Penguin.

Jung, C. (1981). Archetypes and the Collective Unconscious, Princeton University Press.

Tarant, N. (2005). Young Leader, Inkwater Press.

Woodsen, C. G. Mis-Education of the Negro.

www.ingramcontent.com/pod-product-compliance
Lightning Source LLC
Chambersburg PA
CBHW031420210526
45464CB00005B/1972